The ^ Library Meeting Survival Manual

by George J. Soete

Tulane Street Publications • 2000

ISBN: 0-9701384-0-7

Copy Editor: Judith M. Callard
Design: Beyond the Imagination Graphics, San Diego
Printing: SOS Printing Inc., San Diego

Pre-Publication Data

Soete, George J.
    The library meeting survival manual / by George J. Soete.
    144 p. ; 28 cm.
    Practical library management series
    Includes bibliographical references and index.
    ISBN 0-9701384-0-7 (pbk.) : $29.95
    1. Library meetings. 2. Library meetings—Handbooks, manuals, etc.
3. Communications in organizations. 4. Communication in management.
5. Decision making.
Z678.83 2000
025.1–dc21

This is the first monograph in the
Practical Library Management Series

TULANE STREET PUBLICATIONS

Post Office Box 221054
San Diego, CA 92192–1054
1-888-413-8999
Web site: www.georgesoete.com
E-mail: george@georgesoete.com

Table of Contents

Thanks to:

Mary, Judith, Nicole, Steve

Special thanks to all my ARL colleagues,
who have been so generous
with their experiences and insights.

Introduction:

Why This Book?

Why another book on meetings? Hasn't enough been written already? And why a book focusing on **library** meetings?

This book grows out of my experience over the last twenty years as an organizational development consultant specializing in libraries and as a professional facilitator of library meetings of all sorts. During those years, as I listened to the members of client organizations, one theme has been especially compelling: most library staff, from the front lines to the administrative offices, feel they spend too much time in meetings and that the time they spend is often unproductive. There is a litany of unhappiness:

- ◆ Meetings are too frequent and too long.
- ◆ Discussions go on and on, sometimes without apparent purpose.
- ◆ Content is boring, repetitive, unimportant.
- ◆ Sessions start late and run overtime.
- ◆ Agendas are hastily assembled and often unclear.
- ◆ It is rarely clear how and by whom decisions will be made; few substantive decisions are made.
- ◆ Anecdotal content is high and true problem solving rarely happens.
- ◆ A few members may dominate the meeting; others rarely talk at all.
- ◆ There are hidden agendas and political ploys.
- ◆ Action planning is sketchy and follow-up is often nonexistent; there is little or no sense of completion.

In short, for many staff in libraries, meetings represent time wasted—time, they often say, that they could be spending doing their "real work" back at their desks.

I have had another, more visceral experience of library meetings as well. For a quarter of a century, I was, in various incarnations, a staff librarian, department head, and administrator in both academic and public libraries. What I hear from my clients sounds very familiar. For twenty-five years, I was a key actor in the drama—sitting through long, unproductive sessions, taking detailed notes simply to stay awake, and keeping a careful watch on the clock. I have even led such meetings myself!

As I listened to clients and reviewed my own experiences, I began to ponder a series of questions. Why couldn't some of the best, most competent, most dedicated people on the face of the earth—library people—manage meetings more effectively? Why couldn't people who constantly delight and amaze with their ability to organize information—why couldn't these same people organize truly satisfying and productive meetings? Why couldn't libraries, organizations critically dependent on *interdependence,* create the results they needed by working more effectively together? Why were people of talent, good will, and splendid purpose not happier in an activity that absorbed so much of their time?

In fact, that single factor alone—*time*, and the cost it represents—is perhaps the most compelling reason of all for paying attention to meetings. If you estimate conservatively that librarians and library administrators spend a day a week in meetings, for a staff of fifty librarians, the cost for most organizations will approach half a million dollars per year. As a library administrator, I often spent as many as two or three days a week in meetings, not counting one-on-one sessions in my office. Clients often tell me they spend more time than this. Are we spending this time and money effectively? More important, are we holding the kinds of meetings that adequately repay the human effort we put into them? Are we taking advantage of the investment that meetings represent? For many library people, the answer would be *no*.

Obviously, meetings are not the primary business of libraries. Service is. What's wrong with being great at service and not so great at meetings? Indeed, the problem of meetings wouldn't matter if we were not spending so much of our time in them and didn't depend on them so much. Isn't it worth some of our time and effort to improve our management of meetings? My answer is yes. The benefits of effective meetings are many: they help us establish clear, shared directions; they are workshops for crafting ideas and developing programs, and they enhance the success of the group by building commitment to group decisions.

Are Library Meetings Different?

Meetings are a basic human activity. We are social beings. Early humans met to discuss plans for a hunt. Families meet to resolve issues. We meet in board rooms and church basements, lofts, and offices. What's so special about library meetings? The differences lie mainly in the context:

♦ Compared with people in similar fields, library people meet a lot. In fact, I can think of no other type of organization that has more meetings. Part of the reason, I have deduced, is that library people have fewer fixed time constraints. Teachers, for example, spend most of their day in the classroom. And while some library people have fixed commitments on public service desks, for example, most have significant periods of time available for meetings. (I am not suggesting they do not have important things to do, merely that there is a certain amount of flexibility in their schedules.)

♦ Many library meetings are held "just-in-case" rather than "just-in-time." Other organizations would marvel at the capacity of library people to carve out time to attend standing meetings every week, just in case there is something to discuss. The norm in many other kinds of organizations is not to meet unless there is something to meet about. Standing meetings, if they are held at all, are infrequent.

♦ Library schedules and distances between library units often make inclusive meetings—those where all key stakeholders are present—difficult to schedule. The primary example of this is the circulation department in a library that keeps extensive hours of opening.

♦ Many library operations are sequential. Though such structures may be breaking down with the growth of technology, the basic operational sequences such as ordering, processing, and servicing remain in place for a great many staff. To be effective, units must collaborate. The need for interdependence, especially in larger organizations, creates a need for people to meet to inform each other, solve problems together, resolve issues, and make decisions, often across departmental lines.

♦ Many libraries have a number of service points, some of them offering duplicate services. Such an approach calls for constant attention to consistency in policies and procedures, and meetings are a favorite format for discussing and resolving policy issues.

♦ Library people tend to be introverts. This is not just a stereotypical view. When I administer the Myers-Briggs Type Indicator to library groups, the ratio of people who prefer introversion to those who prefer extroversion is typically two to one, while the ratio in the general population is roughly one to one. Introverts prefer quiet introspection and are often less comfortable speaking in groups. The dynamic resulting from this ratio calls for special approaches to meeting management.

♦ Library people like information: it's their business. This means that they can tend to favor the sharing of information during meetings over moving through problem-solving processes toward resolution and decision.

Consideration of these differences led to my decision to write a book focusing on library meetings—one that acknowledges the special circumstances of libraries and proposes realistic strategies for improving library meetings.

Who Should Use This Book?

I believe that improving meetings is everyone's job. Therefore, I have tried to make this book useful to everyone who cares about the quality and productivity of the meetings they attend. Obviously, it is aimed at the department head or team leader who regularly plans and conducts meetings. But it is also aimed at group members who sometimes are responsible for constructing agendas or facilitating meetings. In some groups, all members will share in such responsibilities. Some of the actions that are recommended, such as developing ground rules, need the participation of all members of the group. If all members are working together on the same goal—say, improving agendas—I recommend that they all read and discuss the relevant chapter.

Changing Meeting Habits is Hard Work

How we organize and manage meetings is a social act influenced by powerful norms and models. Our models include entities as widely diverse as football teams, corporate boards, and legislatures. Local history is perhaps the most significant influence of all. Nowhere does the phrase "We've always done it that way" have such power as in meetings, especially standing meetings. Local history often dictates that our meetings have standard, almost ritualistic components: a leader who always chairs the meeting, agendas crammed with topics that provide little information that will help with preparation, thirty minutes (or more!) of information sharing, discussions characterized by speeches rather than true interactions, few actual decisions or actions, and a final rush toward inconclusive endings ("Well, perhaps we've spent enough time on that item for the moment").

When we attempt to improve the status quo, we often try easy methods that appear to address our unhappiness, such as setting time limits on agenda items. When the discussion comes in under the limit, we are satisfied that the new strategy has worked; when it does not, we perceive a failure of members to discipline themselves. Another method is tinkering with meeting times to assure better on-time attendance. Yet another is looking to the leader to act as policeman. What rarely seems to be addressed are the truly fundamental questions:

- What outcomes are you trying to accomplish in your meetings?
- Does everyone understand the overall purpose of your group or your project?
- Does everyone understand how decisions will be made and how and when specific actions will be implemented?
- Are you avoiding the really important business of the group?
- Are you truly listening to one another, or, as is often the case, preparing what you are going to say next?
- Are you including everyone who should be heard?
- Do you have ground rules in place? Do members know the rules about talking too much, straying from the point, dealing with disagreement in civilized ways?

Addressing these issues and making fundamental changes in your meeting behavior is hard work. Not to be over-dramatic, for most of us our meeting behavior has become addictive. Moreover, we have co-dependent relationships in the workplace that strengthen our addiction. One person may see the wisdom of changing, but for change to be meaningful and lasting, critical mass has to be reached. Enough people have to want to change and be willing to work at it to make a difference.

In this book, I assume that you are motivated to make more than superficial changes in your meetings. On my part, I have tried to make the transition to more effective meetings as easy as possible. To help you through the process, I've divided the book into the following sections:

I.   ***Getting Started.*** The next two chapters include a brief overview of meeting concepts and assessment tools that will help you and your group determine how well you are currently doing in meetings.

II.   ***Twelve Actions to Improve Your Meetings.*** This is the core of the book. From a great number of actions that could make your meetings more productive, I have chosen twelve that I think will make a real difference. I have arranged these from those that combine immediate beneficial results with ease of implementation to those that will be more difficult to accomplish but will still produce desirable results. In practice, I'll recommend that you try the first and second actions first, then move down the list, taking time to insure that you give each strategy a fair trial and that it becomes a new habit for you.

III.   ***Tools for Improvement.*** These two chapters include a Checklist that will help you through the whole process of planning and conducting an effective meeting, as well as a selection of "job aids"—an agenda form, task planner, and the like. Permission to copy and use these aids is included in the cost of this book, as long as you use them in the process of improving your meetings and not for other purposes.

How to Use This Book

I encourage you to move around in the book and select whatever looks useful.

However, those who are serious about improving meetings will, after they have completed the assessment, start with the strategies, trying a few at a time and using the related job aids. In the best of all worlds, everyone in a group would approach the problem of improving meetings as a shared learning experience. If the group is going to work on **ACTION ONE**, everyone should read and discuss that chapter. In other words, I am recommending a sort of workshop approach, in which those who meet become *learners and planners*—reading, discussing, making change-oriented action plans, and helping each other through the implementation process toward meetings that are more and more effective. Alternatively, group leaders and facilitators may simply want to use the book as a source of ideas and techniques. I encourage them, however, to share techniques with the entire group, with the eventual goal of everyone taking responsibility for meeting management.

Practice:

If you are going to use this book in "textbook" mode, I have included practice questions and tasks as a way of reinforcing your learning. Here is your first opportunity to practice some of the ideas presented in the book:

1. Compute the cost of meetings in your organization. Start with one group that meets regularly. Estimate the hourly income of members and multiply by the number of hours they spend in meetings per week, month, year.

Section I: Getting Started

This section of the book will get you started on improving your meetings. I recommend that you read it before you go to the core of the book, the twelve recommended actions (Section II). It contains two chapters:

- ♦ ***Meetings 101*** reviews some of the basic concepts about meetings and groups. Though you do not have to be an expert on either topic to improve your meetings, having these concepts in mind as you go about implementing the recommended actions will make the job much easier.

- ♦ ***Diagnosing Your Meetings*** will give you an opportunity to assess your meetings using two different tools. One of these tools is a diagnostic questionnaire; I recommend that everyone in your group complete the questionnaire and discuss the results before the group moves on to consideration of the actions in Section II. A copy of the questionnaire also appears in Section III, ***Job Aids***.

Meetings101:

How and Why We Meet

Meetings are such a common occurrence in many of our lives that we rarely take time to step back and think about them as the truly remarkable social phenomena that they are. As human beings, we work together to get things done, and meetings are one way we work together. Meetings are, in short, a fundamental manifestation of our humanity.

In this chapter, I focus on some of the commonly accepted concepts about meetings and groups to help you build a basic vocabulary. Let's start with a working definition of a meeting:

> ***A meeting is a gathering of persons with the common purpose of accomplishing work together.***

Of course, people gather in other ways to get work done. Construction crews, for example. Meetings have become such a fixture in many of our lives, however, that they have garnered special attention in the literature about the world of work.

Meetings are work. It is the last part of the definition, ***to accomplish work together***, that is the most important. Meetings are primarily vehicles for getting work done. It is when we lose sight of this core purpose that the trouble begins. If we see meetings as events that interrupt our real work, or merely as opportunities to socialize, or as battlegrounds where power is displayed, we are missing the point.

If you take the definition seriously, it will mean that you will treat the meeting place as a work place. You will treat each other as co-workers. You will see the subject of the meeting as the work of problem solving. You will manage the work of the group as efficiently as you manage your own work when you are in control at your work station. It also means that you will begin to understand better the kinds of work that can be done productively in meetings and the kinds that perhaps need to be accomplished in other ways.

Information, Decisions, Feedback. What kinds of work do we meet to accomplish? Meetings are often categorized into three basic types, according to the products that result from them: *information, decisions,* and *feedback.* Sometimes *information* is the principal or sole product. If people are working on a project together but performing the work as separate tasks in separate locations, they may occasionally need to check in with each other about their progress. Or members of an organization may need to stay abreast of current developments in order to do their jobs effectively. Or members may exchange opinions about an issue. In library organizations, many meetings are largely, even exclusively, informational. In part, this may be because the very nature of library work focuses on information. So, sometimes library people have a tendency to see problem solving as largely a matter of gathering and sharing information.

Decision making is, for many meeting-goers, the benchmark of meeting productivity. Decisions can be made during the meeting, as a product of consensus, but they are more typically made after the meeting by the person or persons who have decision-making authority. Sometimes they are made in advance of the meeting, and the meeting is used as a vehicle for informing members about the decision. This can make members of groups feel that meetings have been unproductive: they themselves have not been part of the final decision-making act.

Meetings that lead toward decisions are more likely to be *feedback* meetings, where decision makers are gathering feedback on proposals in order to make the decision at a later date. Project update meetings can also be feedback meetings in which participants report on what they've done, what they are going to do, and seek constructive feedback on their accomplishments and directions.

Just-in-Case, Just-in-Time. There is another way to categorize meetings. Some groups hold meetings at the same time, in the same place, month after month, year after year. I call these standing meetings *just-in-case* meetings; the participants meet just in case they have anything to discuss or decide. Often such meetings have a ritual character. They appear to exist as much to reinforce social bonds as to get work done. Members sit in the same place year after year, and agendas follow a fixed pattern. Other groups meet only when they need to; these are *just-in-time* meetings. Often the difference between just-in-case and just-in-time meetings mirrors the difference between *ex officio* groups such as department heads, the members of a department, and library administrators on the one hand and project or special purpose groups on the other.

Though there is room for both types in the life and work of the organization, the just-in-case meeting is more often the target of complaints. Often there is a mismatch of expectations among group members. The leaders of such meetings might see them as merely informational, a chance to get people together, an opportunity to demonstrate leadership in a visible way. Members of the group, however, might see them as lost opportunities to tackle real issues, solve real problems, and make important decisions.

Just-in-time meetings are often more satisfying because they are likely to be more focused and to deliver more of what participants expect of productive meetings. The business of the meeting is often related to a single objective, sometimes to a single task, making focus much easier. The other positive factor in the just-in-time meetings of project groups is that the project has an end; looming ahead is the prospect that the job will be done and that members can move on to other projects. Participants in just-in-case meetings, especially chronically mismanaged ones, often have, alas, the feeling that they are trapped. One of the key challenges of meeting management, I suggest to clients, is to reduce the number of just-in-case meetings and to make the remaining just-in-case meetings lively, engaging, and productive.

Before and After. When we think about meetings, our tendency is to focus on the event itself, the hour or so that a group spends together. One of the secrets of good meetings is that most of the work happens before and after the specific time during which people are in the same room together or, in an electronic environment, online together. Many of the ideas presented in this book focus on preparing for the meeting (paying attention to the physical meeting space, constructing an outcome agenda) and on follow-up activities (assigning tasks, evaluating meeting effectiveness). Again, it is useful to think of meetings as no different from other work. The meeting is only part of a sequence of tasks that the group is accomplishing, just as a report drafted by an individual is only one part of a sequence of that person's tasks. Poor meeting management typically results from not paying adequate attention to preparation and follow-up. Effective meeting management acknowledges the importance of the before and after, and it can all be done in a surprisingly short period of time if you are organized about it.

Task and Maintenance. When meetings are effective, they are usually the product of both *task* and *maintenance* skills. Task skills focus on the achievement of objectives, the accomplishment of the task at hand. *Maintenance* skills focus on attending to the needs of participants, how they relate to each other, and how they feel about the task. These skills relate directly to the set of expectations that most participants bring to meetings: they want to accomplish the task and they want to relate to each other in effective ways.

Both of these skill sets should be present during effective meetings, and both can be practiced by anyone in the group. Typically, however, our personal styles lead us to prefer one or the other skill. Some people are very good at staying focused on the task. Others are especially good at maintenance skills such as making sure that everyone in the group is heard from and that conflict is resolved.

Balance between these skills is critical. Groups that focus exclusively on task are likely to miss important input from members. Groups that focus exclusively on maintenance (sometimes called process) are at risk for trivializing outcomes.

Group Maturity. Like individuals, groups go through developmental cycles. This cyclical development has been studied and reported on a great deal. Though researchers use different terms for the different stages of group development, the terms I prefer, first used by B. W. Tuckman in 1965, are easy to remember: *forming, storming, norming, performing.* During the *forming* phase, the group is not yet cohesive; individuals are curious, perhaps even anxious about purpose and tasks; they wonder who is in charge, who will make decisions. The *storming* phase is characterized by infighting about values, methods, goals. *Norming* happens when the group develops rules (formal or understood) and resolves the issues that arose during storming. When a group is fully *performing*, it is handling the task and maintenance functions effectively and in balance. When I think of the cycle, I think of four stages of individual development: infancy and childhood, adolescence, young adulthood, and maturity.

What is the point of focusing on the group development cycle? Clearly, when groups are at different stages of the cycle, they will have different needs. Here are some general approaches that may help meeting leaders, facilitators, and participants manage meetings more effectively at the different stages of group development:

Forming Groups. When a group is still forming, meeting managers need to take time in meetings to be sure members understand their charge and their roles and responsibilities in accomplishing the charge. If the person who has created the charge is not in the group, it is a good idea to have a session in which this person joins the group and responds to any questions. Some groups need several clarification sessions before they can get down to productive work.

Storming Groups. Storming groups can be helped by developing ground rules and by using inclusive techniques. In libraries, storming can take fairly subtle forms. Members are not likely, for example, to shout at one another, but they may remain silent or exhibit passive-aggressive behaviors. Even though members might not observe the rules consistently during the storming phase, having the rules available will help move the group toward norming.

Norming Groups. Groups that have just learned how to work together effectively need time to test relationships and behaviors. They also need the latitude of being able to make mistakes. Frequent assessment is an important activity for the norming group. How are we doing? What can we do to make our group and our meetings even more effective?

Performing Groups. Mature groups may seem to need no intervention, but they can backslide every once in a while. Assessment may not have to be so frequent, but taking time occasionally to evaluate how the group is doing will be important. For the performing group, the introduction of new members, a new charge, or new tasks can temporarily push the group back to an earlier phase in the group development cycle.

What are the characteristics of mature groups? What makes some groups effective, while others struggle to understand their charge or to resolve deep-seated issues? Here are some of the characteristics that have been observed in mature groups:

- ◆   *Listening*. Members of mature groups listen attentively and actively to one another. They try to understand other points of view rather than rehearsing what they are going to say next.

- ◆   *Involvement*. In mature groups, everyone participates. Participation is not necessarily evenly distributed, but it is clear that everyone is engaged in the task and is speaking up when they have something to add to the session and volunteering when there are jobs to be done.

- ◆   *Experimentation.* Mature groups try new ideas and approaches.

- ◆   *Accountability and responsibility.* Members take responsibility for getting tasks done and they are mutually accountable for achieving goals.

- ◆   *Trust and caring*. Members trust each other and care about each other. They can talk with each other in forthright, even critical ways without fear of hurting each other. This caring does not overwhelm their relationships, but it does help accomplish the work.

- ◆   *Using subgroups.* Mature groups use subgroups of members to accomplish tasks. They do not feel that every member must be involved in every meeting. They trust each other, and they check in with each other periodically to make sure that tasks are on the right track.

- ◆   *Dealing with differences.* Members can express their differences with each other in civilized and productive ways. They manage conflict creatively.

- ◆   *No hidden agendas.* Members are open with each other. They are in the group to get work done, not to enhance their power or to accomplish secret objectives.

♦ ***Self-examination.*** Mature groups take time to assess their effectiveness, to review mistakes and failures, and to analyze these as learning experiences.

Though it is not essential to understand all the current theories about groups and meetings, it is helpful to have the sort of basic vocabulary presented in this chapter. In my view, all members of a group are responsible for managing their work time together; it has made a critical difference in the groups that I have worked with for everyone to be talking the same language.

Practice:

1. Explore the concepts presented in this chapter by relating them to your experiences in meetings that you currently attend. For example, look at a few recent agendas. How much of the meeting content is informational? How much focuses on decision making, feedback?

2. Consider all the groups you meet with. Do your meetings tend to be just-in-case or just-in time? Are there any meetings that could move from the just-in-case column to the just-in-time column? Would this shift improve the quality of the meetings?

3. Consider two of the groups you meet with, one that has been in existence for a long time and another that has just started. How would you assess these groups on the group development cycle?

4. Identify the most mature group that you currently meet with. How does the group match up against the characteristics identified in this chapter?

Diagnosing

Your Meetings

Do you view your meetings as productive and pleasurable? Or do you dread them, considering them mostly time-wasters? Before you read about the actions that I propose for improving them, take a few minutes to assess your meetings.

This chapter features two assessment tools. The first is a story of two meetings that took place simultaneously on a recent afternoon. After you read the stories, consider which meeting is more like your meetings. The second tool is a questionnaire that describes the major characteristics of successful meetings. You will have an opportunity to rate your own meetings against these measures.

A Tale of Two Meetings

At the Concord University Library and Information Resource Center, all standing departmental meetings are held on Wednesday afternoons at staggered times. With this arrangement, departments can help each other cover public service desks, and personnel on evening shifts who arrive at work in the afternoon are usually able to attend meetings.

Recently, we were able to eavesdrop on two meetings that happened to be held at the same time. Both meetings were scheduled from 2:30 to 4:00.

Reference and Research Assistance Department

Things began badly. Five of the twelve members were late, and the meeting started ten minutes late. When the meeting finally started, the department head asked if everyone had received their agendas on e-mail. Two members said they had not and shifted places so they could look on others' agendas.

The agenda had eight items. The first five items were informational; members had already received the information they needed on four of the items by e-mail. At 2:55, the group reached the fifth informational item. This item took several minutes to discuss. It quickly became clear that this was not an informational item but an issue on which the group would need to make a decision. At 3:15, the item was deferred until the next meeting.

The first announced item of new business, hours of service for the reference desk during the upcoming holiday season, turned out to be controversial. Several people needed to express their opinions on the topic. At 3:45, when all members had declared their opinions on the subject, the department head asked for a show of hands. With seven people for and five people against, the proposal carried. The item was referred to the departmental secretary for implementation.

At 3:50, a member asked if the group could take just a few minutes to discuss her proposal about relocating paper indices to a different part of the reference area. At 4:15, the discussion was still going on, but three members had left the room quietly because of scheduled commitments.

At 4:25, the Department Head declared that the group would need to take up the item under discussion next week, along with the other pieces of unfinished business, which had been deferred from the previous meeting.

Automation Support Department

The meeting started promptly at 2:30, in spite of the fact that two of twelve members did not arrive until 2:35.

One of the members started the meeting. "Today, as you know, we're focusing on staffing for the information desk in the computer lab. I've volunteered to lead the meeting. I hope you've all had a chance to review the summary data that I sent you about lab attendance, peak times, etc., as well as the draft proposal that the staffing subgroup has put together. The key data points and the major items of our proposal are posted on these flip charts so that we can consult them during the meeting. The outcome that we're looking for today is a decision on staffing levels at various hours of opening and a commitment from all of you who staff the desk to support the new schedule. As a later outcome, we may need to draft a request for additional students to help with staffing."

Another member asked who would make the decision. "I was just getting to that," said the meeting leader, turning to the department head. "I'd like this to be a consensus decision," said the department head. "I work the desk just a few hours a week. While I'd like to have some input as a member of the group, you all know the service patterns better than I."

The meeting leader nodded. "Before we start, let's review our ground rules quickly, as well as the results from last Wednesday's meeting evaluation." The meeting leader read through the ground rules, which were permanently posted in the meeting room. The meeting evaluation results had also been posted on a flip-chart sheet. The meeting leader pointed to two items especially. "Let's keep up the good work on ending on time; last week, we had ten minutes to spare. But we also said we need to focus on not critiquing until we've hear all the ideas. Let's get started."

The leader first asked the group if there were any questions or comments about the data they had received. There were three questions, and answers were supplied. The group then turned to the proposal. "The subgroup has been pretty creative in their approach. I'm going to suggest we use the Nominal Group Technique for this discussion. Here are three questions to help you get started, but of course you should bring up any issues that might concern you." The three questions were:

- Is anything in the proposal unclear?
- Are there any fatal flaws?
- Do you have any minor concerns that might lead to tweaking the proposal?

For about ten minutes, each member silently reviewed the proposal and made notes, using the three questions as a framework. Then the leader asked each person in turn to offer one item from her/his list. When all of the questions of clarity had been offered, the group moved on to fatal flaws and then to minor concerns. All of the offerings were listed on flip charts by two members who had volunteered to be recorders before the meeting.

Once all the data were listed, the discussion began. Most items were taken care of through clarification. One "fatal flaw" required a bit more discussion which resulted in a change in the proposed plan. The leader asked, "With these changes, do we have consensus? Can everyone support the new staffing plan?" The answer from the group was yes.

The next item of business was implementation planning. The subgroup agreed to develop a plan within the following two days and submit it to the group by e-mail. The department head spoke up: "Unless something comes up that requires us to meet, I believe we can skip next Wednesday's meeting." The subgroup was thanked. The meeting leader promised to have a summary record of the meeting on e-mail for members before the end of the day.

Finally, the group moved quickly through an evaluation of how the meeting had gone—what worked and what might need to be changed the next time they met. The meeting adjourned at 3:55 p.m.

Key Differences. Two meetings, two different dynamics, and two very different results. What are the key differences?

Reference and Research	***Automation Support***
◆ just-in-case meeting	◆ just-in-time meeting
◆ a crowded agenda with superfluous items	◆ a single-item agenda
◆ no shared desired outcomes	◆ desired outcomes known and announced
◆ late start, late finish	◆ on-time start, early finish
◆ no pre-work assignments	◆ pre-work assignments had been done by all members
◆ meandering process	◆ designed process with separable parts
◆ no announced decision process; decision by vote	◆ consensus process announced at the start of the meeting
◆ discussion characterized by speechmaking	◆ discussion focused on shared clarity, organized problem-solving

♦ next steps not spelled out	♦ next steps identified and assigned
♦ no evaluation of the meeting	♦ brief evaluation

Where are your meetings? Are your meetings more like the first meeting or the second? Are you focusing enough on the *how* of your meetings? Are they time well spent or time wasted? In the next section, you will have an opportunity to respond to a questionnaire that will further help you assess your meetings and identify those areas that you would like to work to improve.

Assessment Questionnaire

In most planning, an analysis of the current situation and the desired future is a critical first step. Where are you? Where do you want to go from here? Before you read any further in the book, I recommend that you complete the assessment questionnaire that begins on the next page. The questionnaire is designed to assess where a specific group is in its meeting effectiveness. Here are a few tips before you begin the assessment:

- ♦ If possible, complete the assessment as a group and talk about the results together.
- ♦ Be honest and realistic. Don't be excessively easy or hard in your assessment. How do you really feel?
- ♦ If you use the questionnaire to assess the meetings of several groups, complete a separate questionnaire for each group's meetings. You have permission to photocopy the questionnaire for such assessment purposes.
- ♦ Another way of using the questionnaire is as a framework for evaluating a specific meeting. The assessment questionnaire also appears in the Job Aids at the end of this book.
- ♦ Consider your own performance within the meetings that you are evaluating, as well as how others perform.

Questionnaire: Consider how often each of the following statements is true of your meetings. Choose **Usually**, **Sometimes**, or **Never**.

	Usually	Sometimes	Never
1. The purpose of our meetings is clear.	_____	_____	_____
2. We have an agenda.	_____	_____	_____
3. The desired outcome of each agenda item is known.	_____	_____	_____
4. Members contribute to the agenda.	_____	_____	_____
5. We have established ground rules.	_____	_____	_____
6. Ground rules are posted and followed.	_____	_____	_____
7. We use a flip chart or whiteboard to record during the meeting.	_____	_____	_____
8. Everyone participates.	_____	_____	_____
9. Our physical meeting space is organized effectively.	_____	_____	_____
10. We keep our meetings on track.	_____	_____	_____
11. Overall, participation is fairly even. No one dominates.	_____	_____	_____
12. We know how decisions will be made and who will make them.	_____	_____	_____
13. At the end of the meeting, members are clear about next steps and tasks.	_____	_____	_____
14. Members follow up on tasks.	_____	_____	_____
15. We meet only when we need to.	_____	_____	_____
16. Members do their homework and complete assigned pre-work.	_____	_____	_____
17. We handle purely informational content outside the meeting.	_____	_____	_____
18. We start and end on time.	_____	_____	_____
19. We use group process effectively.	_____	_____	_____
20. We evaluate how we did at the end of each meeting.	_____	_____	_____
21. We use facilitators, either members of the group or outside facilitators.	_____	_____	_____
22. We accomplish what we need to accomplish in our meetings.	_____	_____	_____
23. We listen effectively to one another.	_____	_____	_____

Now go back through your assessment. Especially note checks in the **Never** column. Which of these items do you feel your group really needs to work on? Note checks in the **Sometimes** column as well. Which five items currently in the **Never** or **Sometimes** columns would make a real difference if you could move them into the **Usually** column?

The questionnaire items reflect the characteristics of effective meetings. Many of these characteristics are reflected in the twelve actions that I recommend in the core chapters of this book. Here they are in summary:

(1)   ***Understand your purpose.*** Often there is a disparity of understanding among group members about the purposes of meetings. What is the overall purpose of your meetings? To get business done? To share information? To reinforce the social bond? Does everyone in your group understand why you meet?

(2,3,4)   ***Develop outcome agendas that everyone contributes to.*** The agenda is the most important planning tool in meeting management. When you put an item on your meeting agenda, do you indicate the desired outcome for the item? Do you want the group to make a decision or do you simply want everyone to understand the issues related to a topic? Shared understanding of where you want to be at the end of a meeting is an important means of keeping the group on track and fostering a sense of accomplishment. It makes the difference between merely wandering about and moving toward a clear goal. **ACTION ONE** focuses on improving your agendas.

(5, 6)   ***Develop ground rules.*** Every group has rules, whether explicit or implicit. Developing ground rules helps the group identify how it wants to manage itself. Can anyone interrupt at any time? How will you handle attempts to dominate the discussion? **ACTION THREE** focuses on developing ground rules.

(7)   ***Record so that all can see.*** Effective meetings happen when the attention is taken away from the participants and placed on the task

or problem at hand. Using flip charts, whiteboards, or other suitable recording media helps direct the group's focus where it should be. **ACTION FOUR** focuses on the flip chart and other recording media.

(8)   ***Include everyone.*** Merely inviting members to participate is not enough. Such invitations can be declined, often for the subtlest of reasons. There are very simple facilitation techniques that promote active participation of those who do not typically participate. **ACTION FIVE** focuses on the use of inclusive techniques.

(9)   ***Pay attention to the physical environment.*** The physical environment has a powerful effect on meeting participants. A room that has been organized to promote productivity will actually aid the group in achieving the work it sets out to do. Furthermore, light, temperature, and noise levels all contribute to the productivity of the group. The physical environment should include all the equipment and supplies that you will need to conduct an effective meeting. **ACTION SIX** focuses on the physical environment of your meetings.

(10)   ***Stay on track.*** For many groups, this is more easily said than done. It seems to be human nature that we sometimes wander about. It takes a great deal of discipline to stop, remind the group of the outcomes they are working toward, and get back on track. Ideally, the whole group will monitor its own progress through the meeting and any member will be able to point out that the discussion is wandering from the point. **ACTION TEN** focuses on techniques for keeping meetings on track.

(11)   ***Manage dominance patterns.*** Some of us talk more than others. Some see the meeting as an arena for exercising power. Fortunately, many of the same techniques that draw out quieter members also help the group manage dominant individuals. **ACTION TWELVE** includes ideas for managing dominance, as well as a variety of other problem behaviors.

(12)   ***Understand how decisions will be made.*** There is nothing quite so frustrating for meeting participants as engaging in a stimulating discussion only to discover at the end that the resulting decision will be made by one person—or that, in fact, it has already been made. Members need to understand whether they are deciding, recommending a decision, or merely providing input into a decision that another will make. **ACTION NINE** focuses on managing the decision process.

(13, 14)   ***Track assignments; end with a clear sense of next steps.*** Clients often tell me that their discussions are interesting enough but that they lack follow-through. Implementation seems to get forgotten. Key next steps need to be identified before the meeting ends, and individuals need to know what their tasks are and when they are supposed to complete those tasks. **ACTION ELEVEN** focuses on following up on assignments and tasks.

(15)   ***Meet only when you need to.*** This is a very difficult idea for many groups, especially those that have regularly scheduled standing meetings. Moving from "just-in-case" meetings to "just-in-time" meetings, however, can really improve the focus and energy of groups. At the very least, the group can decide to cancel regularly scheduled meetings if there is nothing urgent to meet about.

(16)   ***Complete some of the work of the meeting before the meeting starts.*** Often, a great deal of meeting time is taken up with material that can be done by members as pre-work—looking at data, reading proposals, etc. Completing this work before the meeting begins can alert the group to an item's importance and give everyone a head start on the discussion.

(17)   ***Move purely informational content outside the meeting.*** When I look at meeting agendas, I am often struck by how much time is taken up with the review of informational material. Traditionally, this content comes first in the meeting, at the point when presumably the group's energy is highest. Later in the meeting, the

group rushes through, and often does not resolve, the really important issues. If informational content is high, especially when members are hearing it for the third or fourth time, there is a feeling that not much is being accomplished. Reducing the amount of informational content in your meetings is one way of making them more productive.

(18) *Start and end on time.* Time is a commodity that we all have strong feelings about. It is also a great equalizer: everyone, no matter what their job is, has a sense of whether they have spent their time productively or wasted it. Studies have identified chronic lateness as a major source of dissatisfaction for meeting-goers. Punctuality is also, however, one of the more difficult goals to achieve, especially in organizations where individuals have multiple roles, tasks, and priorities.

(19) *Design and use group processes.* Many groups have a very limited process repertoire: presentations and discussion. One of the hallmarks of an organized and productive meeting is the effective use of process techniques such as brainstorming, Nominal Group Technique, and affinity diagraming. Though there are many such techniques, mastering only a few will tighten and focus meetings noticeably. **ACTION SEVEN** focuses on meeting process design, especially on the separation of parts of the process.

(20) *Evaluate your meetings.* Continuous improvement of meeting effectiveness requires that you assess meeting performance regularly. I recommend a quick assessment at the end of every meeting, along with periodic assessments that are more detailed and intensive. Reviewing your assessment of the last meeting at the beginning of the present meeting is crucial to making incremental improvements over time. **ACTION TWO** focuses on evaluating your meetings.

(21) *Use a facilitator.* Entrusting someone with the *how* of the meeting frees participants to focus on the *what*—the content. The

facilitator can be a member of the group (the role can be rotated among members) or an outsider—another staff member, a professional from your parent organization, or an outside consultant. The choice will depend on the needs of the group. **ACTION EIGHT** focuses on using a facilitator for your meetings.

(22)   ***Focus on accomplishments.*** In my view, there is only one valid test of meeting effectiveness. Did you accomplish what you set out to accomplish? That you had a good time, that you ended early, or even that you worked hard—these are not useful measures. Did you do what you set out to do?

(23)   ***Listen!*** Listening is the ***sine qua non*** of effective communication. If you are not really listening to one another and really working at understanding each other, your meetings are guaranteed to fail.

If you have completed your initial diagnosis, it is time to look at the twelve recommended actions in more detail.

Practice:

1. Complete the assessment questionnaire. (It is permissible to photocopy it for this purpose). The questionnaire can also be found in the **Job Aids** chapter at the end of the book.

2. Ask everyone in your group to read this chapter and discuss the two meeting tales. Are your meetings more like that of the first group or that of the second group?

3. Ask everyone in the group to complete the questionnaire. You might even do this online before you meet. Present a tally of the responses, keeping individual responses anonymous. Discuss which areas the group would like to work on.

SECTION II: Twelve Actions
That Will
Improve Your Meetings

The twelve chapters in Section II present twelve actions that you can take to improve your meetings. I have arranged the actions by using classic ease/impact analysis. That is, the actions that will be easiest to implement and have the most positive impact on your meetings are presented first. These actions include changing the way you develop agendas, assessing your meetings regularly, and developing ground rules. Toward the end of the list are actions that will be a bit more difficult to implement and may have positive effects that are less immediate. For example, keeping meetings on track and motivating participants to follow up on assigned tasks can take quite a bit of sustained effort.

A word of caution. The enthusiastic and strongly results-oriented among you may be tempted to implement all twelve actions at once. I recommend starting with **ACTIONS ONE** and **TWO** first. The more ambitious groups might want to add **ACTION THREE** to the kickoff effort. Try these actions for a month or two. Assess how they are working. Make adjustments. When you feel these actions are fully implemented, move on to one or two more actions. Try the actions in sequence if you can, but if you feel that you simply must move quickly to, say, **ACTION NINE** (Clarify the Decision Process), understand that this action will probably be more difficult than the earlier ones and will take more time.

The key action throughout the improvement process will be **ACTION TWO**, regular evaluation. Be sure to take a few minutes at the end of each meeting to evaluate how you are doing in general and how successful you have been in implementing the specific actions you're working on.

Finally, I recommend that all members of the group who will be working on particular actions read and discuss the relevant chapters before they begin work. As with most change, actions that are imposed on a group are not likely to succeed. If all members of the group discuss the ideas and understand why improvements are needed, your chances for success will be much greater.

ACTION ONE:

Change to
Outcome Agendas

One of the easiest and most effective actions you can take to improve meetings—perhaps *the* most effective action—is to change from topic agendas to outcome agendas.

When I train library people in meeting management, I ask them to bring recent meeting agendas with them to the workshops. Inevitably, these agendas are lists of subjects—single words or brief phrases indicating the topics the group will discuss. Sometimes items are even more generic: a single word like "announcements" covers a multitude of meeting sins. Why are members announcing to one another? What objectives are they meeting with these announcements?

Even when they are more specific, topic agendas can be fairly baffling. An example I often use is a topic item I once found on the agenda of a meeting of library managers: "Windows NT." What about Windows NT was this group going to discuss? Installation? Training? Problems? To be fair, most members who attend standing meetings probably have a pretty good notion of what each topic means and where the issue currently is. Such a topic approach, however, invites a rambling discussion. Members are free to translate it as, "We are continuing our discussion of Windows NT, and I can say anything I want, including a number of things I've said already in previous meetings."

When such an item appears for the first time on an agenda, it can provoke endless, time-wasting speculation. Are we thinking about migrating to Windows NT? Has the decision been made already? Are we going to have the NT training we were promised months ago?

And when we seek to improve topic agendas, what we often change is everything but the real problem—the topic format. We set time limits on discussions. Or we refer to the minutes of previous meetings in which the item was discussed. Or we try to make the topics more specific. Yet even when topics are made more specific, they often fail the test of clarity. "Windows NT training" can mean a number of things. Is the training going well or not? Are we going to talk about what staff need by way of training? Are we going to hire a professional to train us, or are we going to rely on in-house talent and expertise?

The problem with topic agendas is the topic format. The topic is merely a label; it does not provide direction or "discipline." It does not tell us where we are going with the discussion. It does not communicate a desired *outcome*. Where do you want to go? What result do you want? In all planning, a sense of the desired outcome is essential.

It is important at this point to draw a distinction between content outcomes and process outcomes. The outcome agenda should focus on *process*, not content outcomes. If you are meeting to decide on the holiday hours of the reference desk, the content outcome would look something like "10:00 A.M. to 4:00 P.M., Monday through Friday." But why would you meet if you already know the content outcome? The process outcome, on the other hand, will look like this: "By the end of the meeting we will have decided on holiday hours for the reference desk."

Why should you use outcomes rather than topics? Knowing where you want to go—where you *have* to go if you have a deadline—is the most powerful tool you have for keeping the meeting on track. As a former reference department head, I know firsthand how discussions about reference desk hours can get sidetracked in myriad ways (reminiscing about how, in the good old days, we used to offer twice as many hours with twice as much coverage or citing what they do in a nearby library system). Such side trips might even be occasionally useful. However, having the desired outcome in front of the group, both on the written agenda and on a flip chart or whiteboard, provides a reference point. The outcome statement says, "This is where we are going. No matter how the journey evolves, we have to arrive here. Even if we have the luxury of scheduling another meeting to finish our discussion, this must be our eventual destination."

Outcome items are relatively easy to construct. The key question is, what do we want to have at the end of the meeting? In the beginning, I recommend using the same opening phrase over and over: "At the end of the meeting. . . ." Or "When our discussion is finished. . . ." Then complete the sentence. For me the completion is most effective when it names or implies an understandable result—a sort of "product." In short, to be truly productive, the meeting must produce a valued product.

The products or outcomes that most often result from productive meetings can take several forms. The outcome may be a decision, or greater knowledge and understanding, or a clutch of creative ideas, or the raw input of everyone in attendance. Projecting the desired outcome helps you to decide what kind of discussion you want to have and what kinds of processes you want to use. Here are some examples of topic items stated as outcome items:

- At the end of the meeting, we will have a decision on hours of opening for the reference desk during the holidays.
- At the end of the discussion, all members will have a greater understanding of the issues related to charging for printing.
- At the end of the brainstorming session, we will have a great many ideas for offering instruction to undergraduates more efficiently. A task group will then take over and draw up a proposed action plan.
- At the end of this participatory session, we will understand the concerns of all the principal stakeholders related to changing our policies on overdue fines. These data will be used by the task group charged with drafting a new policy statement.
- By the end of this meeting, we will have a plan and budget for an internal training program in the new Windows NT system.

Notice that the examples suggest both final outcomes (decisions) and interim outcomes (input, data). In either case, people attending a meeting where the desired outcome is clearly stated are much more likely to stick to the topic and have a sense of accomplishment when they reach their destination.

But who decides which outcomes are desirable and what the outcomes should be? Some outcomes will be obvious, easy to state, and agreeable to everyone in the group. If the holiday season is a month away and the department must announce its holiday hours to its users, stating the desired outcome will not be difficult. In other cases, you may need to have some discussion to define the desired outcome. This can be done at the end of one meeting in preparation for the next meeting, or, briefly, at the beginning of the meeting itself. The meeting is something like a vacation trip: how far do members feel they can comfortably go today? The group may want to go all the way to the final decision or simply to a working definition of the problem.

Practice

1.   Select a topic from a recent agenda and translate it into an outcome statement. Try different sorts of outcomes or "products": knowledge, understanding, decision, creative ideas, input on issues.

2.   Think of a topic that will be on an upcoming agenda. Translate it into an outcome statement. Share it with another person who will be at the meeting and get their reactions.

3.   Try these exercises as a group.

ACTION TWO:

Evaluate Your Meetings

One of the most powerful actions you can take to improve meetings is to begin evaluating them every time you meet. This may seem counterintuitive at first. Evaluate *before* you make improvements? Shouldn't you make improvements and then evaluate whether they are working? Evaluation is so important as a continuing strategy that I recommend that groups begin using it immediately. Before you make improvements, evaluation can help you identify areas of strength and areas to work on. If you continue to evaluate at the end of every meeting, you can track progress. Have you really attacked the problems you need to attack? Where do you need to put in more effort?

The most important reason for starting right away, however, is to begin the process of establishing evaluation as a habit. If you are serious about improving your meetings, you will spend three to five minutes at the end of each session evaluating, and you will continue this process *forever*. In addition, you may want to do longer evaluation sessions periodically, using in-depth discussions or instruments. But the first step is the session evaluation, at *every* session.

The first step in an evaluation process is to establish criteria. These will change over time as your meeting improvement needs change. Criteria can be developed quickly in a group discussion. A list of areas for improvement can be developed by using a combination of idea generation and selection of key criteria. Be careful not to include everything on your list that could possibly be improved about your meetings: such an approach will simply be depressing. Of twenty problems that are identified during the brainstorming session, which are the five that will make a real difference if you make some changes? Thus, a group might identify among their criteria 1) starting and ending on time and 2) not interrupting each other. In choosing working criteria, however, they might identify #1 as a serious problem and #2 as a minor problem that they can return to later.

What do effective criteria look like? For me, they are statements of an ideal state. What will the ideal state look like when you achieve it? Here are a few examples:

- We start and end on time.
- We come prepared; everyone has done the pre-work necessary to get the work of the meeting done.
- We try, as individuals, not to take too much air time.

Though you may find it helpful to use a ready-made list of criteria for evaluation purposes, generating the list yourselves will assure that it will be tailored to the needs of the group and will promote acceptance by members. In fact, this will be a general rule for many processes the group will engage in. What groups create themselves is likely to endure; what they are given is likely to be ignored or shelved.

The most important criterion for evaluating the effectiveness of any meeting has already been established in **ACTION ONE**. Has the desired outcome been achieved? Or, to rephrase the question: Are you satisfied, at the end of the meeting, with whatever result you have produced? Note that the rephrasing incorporates some flexibility. As you discussed the topic during the meeting, you may have discovered issues and problems that were not clear when you started. This discovery may have led you to adjust your desired outcome. Whatever the adjusted outcome, did you achieve it or make progress toward it?

To restate the question as a criterion for evaluation:

"We achieved a satisfactory outcome on each agenda item."

How is the evaluation conducted, once you have the criteria that you want to use? The most effective means, in my view, is to use a few minutes at the end of each meeting to evaluate the session as a group, with everyone providing input. This approach reinforces the fact that everyone in the group is working to improve meetings. I recommend the following steps:

1. Post your shared criteria on a flip chart. If you can, simply leave them posted permanently in your meeting room.

2. Review the criteria quickly at the beginning of the meeting to reinforce for members what the group is working on.

3. Refer to the criteria during the meeting when appropriate. If one of the criteria is to stay on track with discussions and the present discussion has veered wildly off course, anyone in the group should be able to say, "Remember that one of the things we are working on is staying on track; it sounds to me as if we're wandering. I'd like us to get back to the focus we had earlier."

4. At the end of the meeting, use any number of methods during the last few minutes. I recommend the "plus/delta" technique presented below.

5. Whichever technique you use, record the evaluation results briefly on a flip chart and include them in the meeting record.

6. At beginning of the next meeting, review the results of the previous evaluation quickly, along with the criteria. In essence, you are saying, "Here are the goals we are working on, and here is where we are with our work. Looks like we're doing well on this criterion, but we need to pay more attention to this other one."

Plus/Delta

This is an evaluation technique that moves very quickly and can be used at the end of every meeting. The concept is embodied in two questions: 1) What went well during the meeting? and 2) What should we change the next time we meet? Note that the framework is not what you might expect: plus/minus. The emphasis is on change—on desired positive behaviors—not on negative assessment. In practice, anyone can lead the plus/delta session. Using a flip chart, the plus/delta session leader starts with the framework displayed on the next page.

The leader refers to the criteria and asks, "What went well during the meeting? And what changes do we want to make in the future?" Successes are recorded under the plus sign, and desired changes are recorded under the delta. It is critically important that feedback during the plus/delta session simply be heard and recorded. Individuals in the group may have different opinions, but this is not the time to debate or defend. The session leader simply records all input.

If the group agrees, the evaluation can move beyond the criteria, but I would recommend focusing on the criteria first, then asking if anyone has additional pluses or deltas. Periodically, the group might want to mine these additional data for new criteria to add to their list.

Outcome-Based Evaluation

Another approach to evaluation is to focus on desired outcomes. First, review the outcomes. Then members are asked to respond to the following questions:

◆　　Did we achieve the desired outcomes?

Yes ____ No____ Partially____

◆　　What helped us achieve our outcomes?

◆　　What hindered us?

◆　　What should we change/do next time we meet?

Note that, as with plus/delta, there is a focus on positive change.

Evaluation is most effective when you do it every time you meet. Record plus/delta results and quickly review the results from the last meeting at the beginning of each new meeting. Keeping the areas you are working on in front of you at every meeting will be the best way of making needed changes.

Practice

1.　　Think of a problem that your group experiences in meetings. Restate the problem as a criterion—a positive statement of the goal that you feel the group should move toward.

2.　　Consider the most recent meeting that you have attended. Conduct your own plus/delta evaluation of the meeting.

3.　　Develop a list of criteria for your group. Focus on the problems that you most need to work on.

4.　　As a group, conduct plus/delta evaluations of your meetings for at least a month. Discuss the results. Would it be beneficial to use plus/delta every time you meet?

5.　　Try the Outcome-Based Evaluation format, pages 129-130.

ACTION THREE:

Develop Ground Rules

All groups follow rules. All meetings follow rules, whether they are evident or not. Even in total anarchy, there is a hard and fast rule: Anything goes! The third action you can take to improve meetings is to articulate the rules that you want to operate by. Since you already have rules, and these rules are probably not working as well as you want them to, why not craft new rules that are aimed at solving your meeting problems?

Sometimes, group leaders will complain to me about group dysfunctions—both major and minor—and will ask me as an organizational development consultant what to do about them. My perception is that they are asking me to provide them with a magic formula. "What magic words can I say when the group (or an individual member) starts misbehaving that will stop the behavior and return the meeting to sanity?" My immediate response is, "Set ground rules. Let group members know what is expected of them. Better yet, encourage them to set the expectations. Bring everyone into the process of developing the rules and gain consensus on them. Then post them and enforce them."

There are two basic ways of dealing with dysfunctional behaviors in groups— direct intervention and prevention. My preference is always for prevention, and establishing ground rules is the most powerful preventive strategy available to you. Having ground rules does not mean that you will never have to intervene, but the rules are likely to reduce the need for intervention considerably.

Ground rules govern the "how" of meetings. They provide guidance on how decisions will be made, how the group will make sure that everyone has a chance to contribute, and how those who tend to take more air time will be managed. They clarify how the group will manage conflict, interruptions, and latecomers.

The analogy I find most useful in describing meeting ground rules is "pool rules." Everyone is familiar with the concept of rules at public swimming pools: no running, no glass containers, showering before entering—all the behavioral norms that seek to ensure the safety, health, and comfort of everyone using the pool. Pool rules have many virtues. They are short and simply stated, there are not too many of them, and they are *posted* in clear sight. These are all virtues that ground rules for meetings should emulate, in my view. The key difference is that, while there is a fairly standard set of pool rules, meeting participants should custom-design the ground rules that will work best for them.

Developing the Rules. Ground rules can be developed quickly. Here is one sequence that I have used with standing groups:

1.   Ask members to think about the best and worst meetings that they have attended. What are the characteristics of the best and the worst? Members might make contributions like these:

- ♦   "The worst meetings always started ten minutes late."
- ♦   "In the best meetings, we disagreed with each other a lot but it never got personal."

2.   The characteristics are listed in round-robin fashion on two flip chart sheets—one for the best and one for the worst.

3.   From these raw materials, members are asked to develop rules that will be useful to the group. The raw-material examples above might be translated into these rules:

- ♦   We always start on time.
- ♦   We express our disagreement with each other's ideas clearly and respectfully.

4.   Select the rules you want to live by. There will be a tendency at this point to include all of the rules that members have suggested. Remember, however, that, like pool rules, meeting ground rules should be kept brief and memorable. I recommend no more than

ten rules, and they should all fit on a single flip chart sheet.

5.   Post the rules every time you meet.

Alternative Approach.   There is an alternative approach. You can jumpstart the process by providing a few ready-made rules and/or some categories for consideration of the group. A ground rule that I often suggest to clients focuses on confidentiality/attribution. Members agree to a certain level of confidentiality when talking about meetings to outsiders. The rule says that, while they can speak outside the group about the issues and problems the group is working on, they agree not to attribute ideas, quotations, etc., to specific members of the group. This rule serves to provide a safety net for members. They feel they can say what's on their minds without fear of its being attributed to them and spread throughout the organization.

In adopting this alternative approach, you might want to start with a few issues that are particularly problematic for the group. For example, you might develop a ground rule around the issue of starting on time. The group might decide to start at the scheduled time, no matter who is present, and simply expect latecomers to catch up on their own. The point is, decide as a group what you want the rule to be—and don't cater to the lowest common denominator (that is, the chronic latecomers). Once members begin to understand that the meeting is an important part of their work day, they will begin to improve their on-time performance.

Here is a list of areas that might prompt the group in developing ground rules:

- ◆   confidentiality/attribution
- ◆   starting and ending on time
- ◆   making sure that pre-work is done
- ◆   taking too much air time
- ◆   expressing disagreement
- ◆   participation, too little or too much
- ◆   managing a level playing field
- ◆   how decisions will be made

What do effective ground rules look like? Once again, any rules that the group comes up with in a thoughtful process are likely to be the most effective. To an outsider, the group's rules may look crude, or overpowering, or underpowered, but the rules *belong to the group* and this is the key to their effectiveness. Having written those words, however, I'll suggest a few guidelines:

1.   Keep the rules brief and few in number. The rule of thumb might be that any member of the group will be able to recite the rules without aid of a written document. Ten or fewer rules are ideal.

2.   Use positive statements that indicate preferred behaviors whenever possible. "Be on time and ready to start working at the announced meeting time" clearly indicates what is expected.

3.   At the same time, feel free to use negative statements as a vivid way of discouraging certain behaviors. Often, with the well-intentioned purpose of encouraging positive behavior, we create unclear, convoluted statements of our behavioral expectations. At the pool, "No running!" is much more effective than "Walk at a safe rate of speed." "No pagers, beepers, or other outside interruptions!" sends a clear message about an issue that is a growing problem in today's organizations.

What if the group will have a short-term existence—a project group, for example? Is it worth taking the time to develop ground rules? My answer is yes, though the process and product will probably look a bit different. In this instance, the group leader might provide a few ready-made rules for discussion and revision and invite members to add other rules to the list.

Practice:

1.   On your own, think of the characteristics that you have noticed in both the best and worst meetings. Translate these, just for practice, into ground rules. See an example on page 134.

2.   Invite a group that you currently meet with to develop ground rules. Offer to lead the ground rule session with the group.

ACTION FOUR:

Use a Flip Chart

Meetings are problem solving sessions. Even in purely informational sessions, we are trying to solve the problem of ignorance. As they work through the classic problem solving cycle, participants in a meeting need to develop a shared definition of the problem, generate data and creative ideas together, develop criteria and assess options, choose actions, and plan implementation. I am constantly amazed at the tendency of many groups to perform these very sophisticated processes without shared visual referents—without recording the working out of the problem in a medium that is accessible to everyone in the session. They prefer simply to talk, with the problem seeming to float somewhere in the air between them. Think about it: no mathematician would feel comfortable talking with others about a problem without a piece of chalk and a chalk board at hand.

ACTION FOUR, therefore, suggests that you use a flip chart or two every time you meet. There are many benefits to flip-charting, and nearly all of them can be achieved with a whiteboard, chalkboard, overhead transparency, LCD panel, or virtually any technology that enables everyone present to see what is being worked on. Whiteboards and chalkboards cannot be carried away and transcribed, however, and they are subject to erasure. Other media are dependent on working electronics. Yet, though flip charts are preferred, finally the shared visual experience is more important than the medium.

What are the benefits of flip charts?

1.   The primary benefit, in my view, is that the flip chart focuses everyone's attention on the problem arena and consequently takes the focus away from interpersonal dynamics. There are, of course, times when the interpersonal content is important. At those times, you can move the flip

chart aside and talk things out. But most meetings are about getting work done, and the flip chart helps us focus on the business at hand.

2. Flip-charting promotes shared problem solving and decision making. It reduces re-work and revisiting decisions. Everyone sees the problem being worked out and agrees, "Yes, this is the problem. These are the possible solutions we came up with. These are the criteria we developed together. This is the solution we decided on, complete with the modifications we made. And here is the implementation plan—who will do what, by when, and by what means." If the flip chart record has been effective, members will leave the meeting with a clear sense of where they are and what needs to be done next.

3. The flip-chart record, usually with a bit of amplification, becomes the record of the meeting. There is no need for anyone to take separate minutes. An important tip: the flip chart sheets should be transcribed and the ideas amplified as soon as possible after the meeting while their meaning is still fresh and clear. Also, it is not advisable to hand transcription off to someone who was not at the meeting; they will often not understand the content sufficiently.

4. The flip chart provides a visual tool for keeping participants on track, particularly if you have started the meeting by writing the desired outcome on the first page.

5. Ideas can often be presented more effectively in graphic form. It doesn't require an artist's skill to liven up a discussion with a simple pie chart or an impromptu process flow chart.

I have indicated at the beginning of this section that flip-charting is a bit more difficult than the previous actions; this is partly because there is a modest initial cost for supplies. Here is the basic supply list:

♦   At least two sturdy flip-chart easels. There are some excellent collapsible and portable models available for less than $100. There is no need to spend a great deal of money for elaborate easels.

In fact, you can get along without easels altogether if you have enough wall space in the meeting room for the posting of flip-chart sheets.

- ◆ Pads of flip-chart paper. Invest in full size pads, not smaller artists' sketch books.

- ◆ Flip-chart marking pens in assorted washable colors. Do not use permanent markers or dry markers meant for whiteboards.

- ◆ Masking tape or drafting dots for posting sheets on the wall. The latter are friendlier to wall surfaces.

There is another reason that flip-charting is a bit more difficult than the previous strategies. I have occasionally met with resistance to them. For some participants they seem to have a negative impact, representing approaches that they have had bad experiences with. A friend of mine put these feelings in a very vivid way:

> "Oh no! We are all going to brainstorm and have all the dozens of ideas written on flip charts and then stuck up all over the room. And I bet afterwards the flip-chart pages will go in the trash and we'll have wasted a whole day. Why don't we just sit down and analyze the problems and come up with solutions? Or better yet, I could do it sitting alone at my desk."

These feelings bring up an important rule of effective meeting management:

> ***Never let a tool substitute for real work, real problem solving, or real decisions.***

Any tool can be used for the wrong purposes. Flip charts are simply tools. They should always be subordinate to the real reasons you are meeting—to solve problems.

Tips for the recorder. Flip charts are, in my experience, foolproof, low tech tools, but there are still some techniques that will make your use of them more effective:

1. Use bold, darker colors. Use lighter colors only for highlighting.

2. Try to transcribe accurately. If you are uncertain that you have heard what someone has said, ask them if what you have written down accurately reflects their idea.

3. Keep the flip chart or other surface within view of all members. Stand to the side to write. If you have to stand in front of the flip chart to write, step aside quickly after you've written.

4. As you fill up sheets, tear them off the pad and post them on the wall with masking tape or drafting dots. The goal is to have all the important ideas and actions available for everyone to see. To save time, ask one of the group members to "tear and tape."

Practice:

1. Select a group that is open to change. Invest in a pad of flip-chart paper, a box of pens, and a roll of masking tape. Start using the flip chart in your meetings. Use it at first for simple tasks—developing ground rules or listing brainstorm ideas. You can always expand your repertoire. Get input from members.

2. The next time you visit a business supply store, price flip-chart easels, pads, markers, and so forth. Prepare a budget for the supplies you need to add flip-charting to your meetings.

ACTION FIVE:

Use Inclusive Techniques

One of the questions clients frequently ask me is, "How can I get people more engaged in meetings? How can I stimulate participation?" This is a very sophisticated question, as it signifies an understanding that engagement in the collective work of the organization is an important sign of commitment to organizational goals.

When group members are not participating, what is going on? Why do they appear sometimes to lack energy, to be uninvolved? I believe that most people who attend meetings want to have a good experience. They want the group to accomplish its purposes and they want to contribute. I am convinced that what we perceive as passive lack of involvement in meetings is often *learned* behavior. Members learn over time, often through subtle signals, that they are expected merely to receive and accept information and decisions and that they ultimately have very little influence in the life of the organization. (Whether this is the intended message or not is, in a way, beside the point.) Such behavior is typically verbalized in this way, "I am not being paid to make the decisions. That's management's job. Therefore, my role is to listen carefully and try to take accurate information back to the people who will need it." To me, this is just a mask. What the person is really saying is, "I would like to be involved, to contribute, but what's the use? I've tried to make a difference and no one listens to me." It is critically important that leaders believe that participants want to be involved, since inclusion and involvement are key ingredients of more effective meetings.

Using inclusive techniques that foster the engagement and commitment of meeting participants is **ACTION FIVE**. You may ask, "Isn't it enough that the person has been invited to the meeting and has a chance to ask questions and make comments?" In fully evolved, high-performing groups, this may indeed be enough. In such groups, members trust each other and have a history of productivity together. They naturally fall into a participative mode, giving and taking ideas and opinions freely. Most groups, however, need more than just the implied invitation to participate; they need an inclusive structure and activities that are designed to bring them in.

How to Include Everyone

Though it will take some adjustment and effort, using inclusive techniques is not difficult. You will be a bit ahead of the game if one or more members of the group have facilitation skills and experience, but the techniques offered below are within the grasp of anyone.

Inclusion in the agenda building process. Start by including members in the development of agenda topics. By this, I mean more than the standing, pro forma call for topics that goes out in advance of many meetings. One approach is to start building the agenda for the next meeting at the end of the present meeting. "What should we work on next time?" is a logical question. Another is to ask participants to review and revise the preset agenda at the beginning of the meeting.

Prioritizing the agenda is a rare practice in meetings but an effective means of involving members. "What's most urgent and important for us to start with today?" is the key question. Just as individuals can prioritize the activities of the day ahead of them, so groups can prioritize their work during a meeting. What should be done right away? Do we need to decide about X before we start talking about Y?

In short, if members have been involved in the development of the agenda, in the identification of problems to work on, and in the prioritizing of agenda items, they are more likely to participate with energy and commitment.

Once the group has identified the agenda topics, ask members to share in the development of outcome statements (see **ACTION ONE**). This can be done during agenda building for the next meeting or even at the beginning of a session.

52

Leading Discussions. Ask members to take responsibility for leading discussions. Many meetings consist of what I call "talking heads." The group's formal leader (chief librarian or department head) presides, often developing the agenda and prioritizing it in advance. The leader opens a topic and members who are sufficiently motivated make speeches about it. Such a process is not conducive to real listening and to movement toward results. To change this pattern you need to break away from some ingrained habits.

Ask individuals to lead different parts of the meeting, perhaps even making a brief presentation from a flip chart on the facts and issues before the discussion begins. Such discussion leaders do not have to be subject experts who present topics only in their areas.

Brainstorming. Use idea generation techniques such as brainstorming to stimulate energy and involvement in the group. Anyone can run a brainstorming session. First the facilitator reviews the "rules" of brainstorming briefly with the group (it is useful to have these posted, by the way):

- ◆   Members call out ideas.
- ◆   There is no discussion or critiquing of the ideas.
- ◆   Wild and creative ideas are encouraged.
- ◆   All ideas are written down on a flip chart by the leader or by a scribe.

Then the facilitator poses a question to stimulate ideas. "How can we encourage better attendance at our training sessions?" Or, "What are all the possible ways that we can publicize the upcoming changes in our overdue policies?"

The goal is to develop a great deal of data very quickly. To do this, the facilitator has to be both disciplinarian and cheerleader. As groups are learning to do brainstorming, there will be a tendency to evaluate ideas and to want to discuss them during the brainstorming phase. The facilitator needs to remind them that evaluation and discussion will come later. Also, at the beginning, groups may be relatively quiet, perhaps even reluctant to offer ideas. The facilitator can help by encouraging participation and being patient. Sometimes silence can be frightening, but a brief period of silence might be just what is needed for the group to move into its most creative phase.

Once a list of ideas has been generated, the group can begin discussion and evaluation. I like to use a few criteria to frame such discussions. "Which of these ideas do you feel are both feasible and would help us toward our goal?" You can use sophisticated tools like the criterion matrix, but I find that simply starring the best ideas usually works well.

With such a process the typical pattern has been broken. Everyone is involved and the outcome is the product of many minds, not just a few.

Nominal Group Technique. This is a favorite of mine for involving everyone in the group. Like brainstorming, it is basically an idea generation technique, but it has a very different feel. It is particularly effective in working with library people, many of whom prefer to think quietly and write their thoughts down before offering them to the group. It is also a useful technique when the issue to be discussed will be a bit difficult for the group. The steps are these:

- ◆ The facilitator announces a topic and a question. "We seem to be having some difficulty coming to resolution on the new policy. Let's take a few minutes to identify all the issues that people have on their minds."
- ◆ Members then work quietly and independently, writing issues down on their yellow pads.
- ◆ When everyone is finished, the facilitator asks members, one by one in round-robin fashion, to offer their ideas.
- ◆ Each idea is transcribed on the flip chart. (It may take several flip-chart pages to record all the ideas).
- ◆ Ideas are not critiqued or discussed during the listing phase.
- ◆ Duplicate ideas should be recorded, as I often find that the assumed duplicate actually puts a somewhat different twist on a previously stated idea.
- ◆ Once the ideas have been listed they are reviewed for clarity. It is important here not to move into evaluation or discussion but merely to give members an opportunity to clarify ideas.
- ◆ Once all the ideas are clear to everyone, evaluation and discussion

can begin, as recommended under Brainstorming above.

The Nominal Group Technique is a much more orderly, structured process than brainstorming. Ideas also tend to be more fully stated since members take time to write them down before offering them.

Divide into Small Groups. Anyone who has attended a workshop or two has probably been asked to join a small group for discussion at some point. One of the reasons trainers use this technique is to promote greater participation among learners. Small groups are much more comfortable for members who are otherwise reluctant to speak in the full group.

I have asked groups as small as five or six in number to form smaller subgroups. It is an especially useful technique when the meeting is scheduled to be somewhat longer and the content may be intense. Members seem to be grateful for the break in routine, and the energy level rises perceptibly. Here is a recommended process, though in time you will feel comfortable using your own variations:

♦ Subgroups should be diverse, if possible. The ideal group will have people from different functional areas and different levels of the organization.

♦ Subgroups work best when they have a task. Sometimes, I even suggest that they use simple worksheets. Of course, the task should focus on accomplishing something worthwhile. All groups might work on the same task, or each might work on a different task or a different aspect of the same task. Here are some examples of tasks that small groups might work on:

• Idea generation. All the subgroups might work on the same problem, as in brainstorming and Nominal Group Technique above. Members of a cataloging team might generate ideas on how to tackle a backlog or how to reduce per item cataloging time.

• Data gathering. Members of a staff training group might be asked to list perceived training needs among staff. One group might focus on automation skills, while another focuses on the so-called softer skills—communication, conflict management, etc.

- Issue exploration. Groups might be asked to explore the pros and cons of a tentative decision and suggest ways to make the decision more effective.

- Implementation planning. Small groups might be asked to list the requirements for implementation of a project. Different groups might take on different parts of the implementation plan: personnel, equipment and supplies, etc.

♦ Subgroups should record their work on flip charts.

♦ When the groups are finished with their tasks, each reports to the larger group on the outcomes of its discussion.

♦ At this point, the larger group can look for common ideas and themes among the subgroups' reports, identify items for further work, etc.

Take it Seriously. There is one important point to remember about inclusive techniques—in fact about any of the techniques that you might use to improve meetings. ***You must be serious; the processes must be genuine.*** Meeting participants are uncanny at detecting what I call "cosmetic processes"—processes that look good but are not really intended to lead anywhere meaningful. If, for example, you are not going to take the product of brainstorming seriously, don't do brainstorming.

On the other hand, the benefits—perhaps even the joy—of using inclusive processes authentically will be noticed quickly in the increased energy of the group and the higher overall quality of meeting outcomes.

Practice:

1. Review some old agendas from your files. Look for opportunities in the agendas to use inclusive processes. Try applying a couple of different process options.

2. Review the next agenda for a meeting that you attend regularly. How

might inclusive processes be used to liven up the meeting and stimulate greater participant involvement?

3.   At an upcoming meeting, preferably one in which there is a high level of trust and good will among members, suggest that you would be willing to facilitate an inclusive group process.

ACTION SIX:

Improve the
Physical Environment

One of the key discoveries of the 20th century was that the physical environment in the workplace is critically important. It is no less important in the workplace that we call the meeting room. Some environments are conducive to productivity and others are positively depressing. **ACTION SIX**, therefore, focuses on improving the physical environment in which you meet.

The physical environment encompasses space, furnishings, equipment, and the relationships of people within the space. Meeting environments do not have to be deluxe, but they should meet standards of comfort and they should be equipped for the work at hand. Here are some recommendations for improving your meeting place as a physical environment.

Clear the Decks. The first step in improving a meeting space is to focus on it as a work place—a place where work will be accomplished. For many spaces, this means doing some housecleaning. As a consultant, I have worked in meeting rooms that looked more like used furniture stores than places of work. The first order of business should be to remove all unnecessary furnishings and equipment. Though it is tempting to use meeting rooms as storage areas, clutter such as old computer terminals and retired furniture should be removed ruthlessly. If you don't want it in your personal work space, then it doesn't belong in the meeting room either. Have only enough chairs and tables in the room for the maximum number of participants that you are likely to have in any meeting; store extra chairs somewhere else.

Clear the Walls. Second, clear the walls of all unnecessary decoration. If possible, retain a wall clock only. This is not a puritanical edict but a practical move; you will want as much free wall space as possible for the posting of flip charts. You may also want to post as permanent fixtures such items as group ground rules. If you can get the walls painted, so much the better. Invest in a large whiteboard. I recently worked in a meeting room that had an entire wall, floor to ceiling and corner to corner, covered with whiteboard. We were able to use the wall to map out a complete staff development program.

Invest in Needed Equipment and Supplies. In **ACTION FOUR**, I recommended that you invest in flip charts, easels, pens, and tape or drafting dots. For me, this is essential equipment for any meeting, and it requires an investment of only a few hundred dollars. You may also want to invest in an overhead projector if you plan to use transparencies in meeting presentations. More than this is purely optional. There are many marvelous, usually inexpensive, pieces of equipment on the market, but my own preference is not to focus on the technology but rather on the low tech capabilities that will get the job done.

Consider the Furniture. Many meeting rooms are blessed (or cursed!) with large, heavy tables which may be a beloved part of the organization's heritage but are really relics of the bad old habits of meeting management. In subtle ways, they symbolize command-and-control management systems and all the power and authority that goes with them. In standing meetings, participants often take the same places at the table year after year, with the group leader firmly ensconced at the head of the table. Similarly, meeting room chairs are often excessive: they swivel and roll and have imposing high backs. If you are able to design or redesign your meeting room, go for flexibility and lightness. Smaller collapsible tables that can be joined together or separated, depending on your need, are ideal. When the group is smaller, some of the tables can be folded away and stored. Chairs tend to be a more personal choice; if you are able to purchase new chairs, let members try out samples and have input into the decision. A mixture of chair types within the same style and color scheme is a good idea. For example, some people prefer arms on their chairs and others have no preference. There are excellent resources available on ergonomic standards for chairs.

Change the Seating Arrangement. The most important ingredients of any meeting, of course, are the people. The typical arrangement of participants in a meeting is around a rectangular table with the group leader at the head of the table, much as the head of a nuclear family in the 1950s would preside at Sunday dinner. The advantage of such an arrangement, we are told, is that everyone can see everyone else and discussion will flow more easily. I have a different view. Participants should be oriented not toward each other but *toward the problem or task that they are working on.* They should have easy access to one another, of course, but the primary focus should be on the task at hand and the desired outcome.

In **ACTIONS FOUR** and **FIVE**, I recommended using recording media that everyone can see and calling on all participants to share in the leading of meetings. One of the best ways to accomplish these actions is to identify an area for displaying work and focus attention in that direction. This may be a whiteboard , flip chart, transparency, or PowerPoint presentation, and it may be anywhere in the room. It can shift as the tasks shift. Critical to this sort of flexibility, however, is the ability of participants to shift themselves physically to focus on the task area.

Temperature, Light, and Sound. Unfortunately, meetings are often sedentary events, causing some participants to feel uncomfortably chilly after a while. Room temperatures should be adjustable therefore. I prefer lots of light and little or no extraneous noise in meeting rooms. If you can meet in a suitable room with windows, by all means do so. As we now know, many people are positively affected by natural light.

Change the Venue. We are told by change gurus that stability is as important as change in the life of an organization. However, making changes once in a while in meeting environments can be quite stimulating. One kind of change is to move the meeting to a different room—out of the main library and into a branch, for example. Another is to encourage participants to sit in different places at every meeting. Such physical changes can promote different ways of looking at problems and issues.

Practice:

1. With your group, conduct an inventory of your usual meeting place using the following checklist:

    ♦   Does the room have just enough furniture and equipment for the meetings that are held there or is there excess "stuff" that should really be moved out?
    ♦   Are the walls clear and useable as surfaces for flip charts, etc.?
    ♦   Is the furniture light and flexible? Can it be folded or stacked and stored?
    ♦   Are chairs comfortable? Portable?
    ♦   Is the room equipped with flip charts? A large whiteboard? Pens, tape, etc.? Overhead projector (if needed)?
    ♦   Are you able to adjust lighting and temperature for comfort?
    ♦   Is the room acceptably quiet, i.e., free of extraneous noise?

2. Evaluate how participants are seated during your regular meetings. Does the setup encourage them to focus on each other or on the task at hand? What adjustments could you make to place the focus more squarely on the task and yet enable them to see each other?

3. Evaluate your meeting habits with regard to location. Do you always meet in the same room? Do participants always sit in the same places during meetings? Explore other options for your group: are there other locations where you could meet for a change of pace? Other ways of arranging your meeting room?

ACTION SEVEN:

Design the Process

In this chapter, I recommend an approach to meeting design that has been strongly implied in earlier actions: designing the process. I also recommend separating parts of your meeting process. These are very powerful approaches to meeting management, but they do require some planning and a bit of facilitation skill.

The process that many groups use to get their work done is often haphazard. The agenda topic is announced, participants start talking, and eventually the group may arrive at a suitable destination, such as an increase in information, a decision, or an action plan. Along the way, they may, after a fashion, use different processes. The difference in the action recommended here is that you will be designing the process in advance. Clearly, no process design should be followed blindly, but thinking about process stages before the meeting and then keeping them separate during the meeting can provide a focus and productivity that you would not have otherwise.

Process 101. Experts tell us that there are really only two products in meetings: information and decisions. While real life meetings may not be so simply analyzed, it is a useful enough distinction for our purposes. In addition, there are basically two kinds of processes, based on two different mental modes or problem solving methods: *divergent* and *convergent*.

- ♦   *Divergent processes* reflect the mind in its open, accepting mode. What are all the possibilities, including the wild and crazy ones? Brainstorming is a divergent process.

- ♦   *Convergent processes*, on the other hand, reflect the mind in its evaluative, selective, and decisive mode. Of all the possibilities before us, which are the ones that meet our criteria and which is the one that we will finally choose? Decisions are usually the result of convergent processes.

If you look at divergence and convergence as complementary processes, they are very much like the process used by professional photographers. Professionals shoot many rolls of film (divergence) from which they select only one or two shots (convergence).

Informational Sessions. When the desired outcome is information, process design can be relatively simple:

- ◆   Information is presented.
- ◆   There may be questions and a discussion.

Even when the process is straightforward, however, you may want to think about design. Do you want to move through the presentation first and hold questions and discussion, or will it be more effective to take questions and allow discussion at any point in the presentation? Allowing the presentation to move forward in an unimpeded manner can be effective, especially if the presenter anticipates questions or concerns that are likely to come up. At the same time, longer presentations might be effectively broken up by opportunities for discussion and questions at predetermined intervals.

Decision Sessions. Decisions are typically the product of problem solving. If you think of a decision session as following the classic six-stage problem solving process, it is easier to see how the session can be divided into separate parts. Without such divisions, the group may go astray, rushing ahead to solutions before problems are satisfactorily defined, lingering too long on data gathering or idea generation, or skipping detailed implementation planning altogether.

In the classic problem solving model, the six stages are:

1.   Identification/Definition of the Problem(s).
2.   Data Gathering.
3.   Idea Generation.
4.   Analysis of Data and Ideas; Deciding.

5.   Action Planning.

6.   Follow-up and Evaluation.

Of course, decisions can be made without using every step in the process, but if a decision is important enough to meet about, it is probably merits use of the whole process.

Each stage of the problem solving process can be divided into divergent and convergent sub-processes. Here is how it might look generally:

1.   Identification/Definition of the Problem(s).

  ♦   **Divergent.** Open discussion involving all participants. How is this a problem? Whom does it affect?

  ♦   **Convergent.** What is the specific problem that we must deal with? The task is to narrow the problem to what is really worth spending time and resources on.

2.   Data Gathering.

  ♦   **Divergent.** What data might we find useful in solving this problem? The task is to identify all possible data that you might want to gather.

  ♦   **Convergent**. Which data are critical to solving this problem? Which data are easy to find? The task is to make the data gathering as efficient and effective as possible.

3.   Idea Generation.

  ♦   **Divergent.** What are all the ways that we might solve this problem—even the crazy ways? The task is to generate a mass of both ordinary and creative ideas.

  ♦   **Convergent.** Which possible solutions will we choose for further analysis and discussion? The task is to do a preliminary sort so that the idea list is more manageable.

4.   Analysis of Data and Ideas; Deciding. Analysis implies convergence, so the sub-processes here are convergent.

  ♦   **Convergent**. What are the key messages in the data? The task is to select the data that will lead us toward the best decision or solution.

- ♦ **Convergent.** Knowing what we now know about the problem, what criteria should we use to evaluate the solutions that we have generated? The task is to establish a rational basis for the final decision.
- ♦ **Convergent.** Which solution best meets our criteria? Which is within our capabilities? Which will most effectively solve our problem? The task is to narrow the possibilities to a rational choice.

5. Action Planning.
- ♦ **Divergent.** What are all the actions we might need to take to implement this decision? The task is to make sure that the implementation plan includes everything required to make it successful.
- ♦ **Convergent.** Which actions will we choose to carry out, how will we organize them, to whom will we assign them? The task is to develop a detailed action plan that is both time- and cost-effective.

6. Follow-up and Evaluation.
- ♦ **Divergent.** What are all the possible ways we could assess whether the implementation process is on track and whether the solution meets the criteria we set earlier?
- ♦ **Convergent**. How will we actually evaluate implementation and make sure actions are accomplished? The task is to develop a detailed follow-up and evaluation plan, with assigned responsibilities, timetable, etc.

In other words, as the group accomplishes its work, there is a continuous oscillation between broad and narrow focuses—between divergence and convergence. The entire process may take an hour, or it may take several weeks.

Though you may not need to use the full-blown process outlined above, with all of its sub-processes separated, the key message is to look for separations that make sense. It is perhaps clearer to talk about what happens when the group *fails* to separate the parts of the process. In the idea generation phase, for example, if you do not separate sub-processes you are likely to simply throw out ideas one by one, discussing and evaluating each one as it comes up, rejecting several ideas out of hand. When a particularly attractive idea turns up, the group may choose it without further discussion and begin implementation planning pretty much as the idea was proposed. When you separate the sub-processes, on the other hand, you first look at all the possibilities; you do not discuss, evaluate, accept, or reject any of them. When you see all the possibilities first, discussion and evaluation are richer. A standalone idea that you would otherwise reject out of hand might influence the shape that another idea takes. Ideas grow and build on each other when they have the space that divergent processes provide.

The Discipline of Separation. Separating sub-processes requires great discipline. The natural tendency is to want to talk about the "raw data" before they are all assembled. This is where a discussion leader or facilitator is useful. Part of this person's job is to remind the group of the present focus, especially if it is divergent, and to remind members that they will have an opportunity for questions and discussion later.

Testing for Resolution. When I train people in facilitation skills, I offer a rule: *Never end on a divergent sub-process!* For example, never stop your work after you have brain-stormed a list of ideas. Some groups do not seem to get beyond divergence. Clients have told me, "We make great lists, and then we never hear about the issue again." Divergence without convergence can be very frustrating for members of a group. To avoid this frustration, always test for resolution. "Have we reached the decision we needed to reach? Do we all have a sufficient understanding of the real problem to move on to data collection?"

Practice:

1.   Look at some past and future agendas for groups that you belong to. Can you identify the items that are informational and those that are decision items?

2.   From the same agendas, choose a decision item. If you were to

design a process for this item following the six-step problem-solving model and moving between divergent and convergent modes, what would the process look like? Take time to sketch it out in some detail.

ACTION EIGHT:

Use a Facilitator

All of the actions recommended so far focus on meeting process. In this chapter, I suggest that you use a process facilitator—someone who helps the group with the *how* (process) of the meeting rather than the *what* (content).

Facilitators can be members of the group, members of the larger organization who are not group members, or persons from outside the organization who are working either gratis or for pay. Most facilitation can be handled inside the group. When group members facilitate, however, I recommend that this responsibility be rotated and shared among all members and not simply carried out by the group leader.

When do you need a facilitator? My answer is, *every time you meet.* In very mature, high-performing teams, you may not need a facilitator all the time, but even in these cases a facilitator might be a very important addition to some meetings.

What do facilitators do? As noted previously, facilitators focus on the process of the meeting. They manage the process so that everyone else can focus on the content. Here is a list of contributions that a skilled facilitator can make:

- Lead the group through processes such as agenda setting, development of ground rules, brainstorming, and task planning.
- Record ideas and decisions on flip charts or other media. (Some groups like to have a recorder as well as a facilitator; in my own practice, I tend to facilitate and record.)
- Keep the group on track by reminding them of desired outcomes and time constraints.
- Encourage participation through process design, as well as through mild interventions.

- Safeguard ideas. It is normal for members to critique ideas as soon as they come up; the skilled facilitator reminds the group that all ideas deserve a fair hearing. Ideally, every group would have a ground rule related to the safeguarding of ideas.

- Maintain neutrality. Especially when there is disagreement in a group, a facilitator can be an welcome oasis of neutrality for members. At the same time, maintaining neutrality can be a real challenge, especially for facilitators who are also group members. But it is perhaps obvious that in some situations the very person who is supposed to be helping the group with process should not also be getting into content, taking sides, or evaluating member contributions.

- Suggest methods and techniques. Accomplished facilitators often have a toolbox of techniques and models, but it is possible to be an effective facilitator without a huge technical repertoire. In my own practice, I tend to use a few tried-and-true techniques over and over.

- Intervene in certain kinds of meeting behaviors—for example, dominance.

When should you use an outside facilitator? For most situations in most groups, facilitation can be provided by group members. There is a problem with internal facilitation, however, when the facilitator has to wear two hats—both as a neutral helper and as a member of the group concerned with the content. With some practice, members will be able to balance these two roles in most situations. But there are situations when you will want all group members focusing on the content. This can happen when the content is very important and may lead to disagreement among group members. Some content simply demands the full attention of all members; it would be unfair, in fact, to ask someone to facilitate a session, especially to try to maintain neutrality, when that person has a significant stake in the session outcome.

How do you select a facilitator? If the facilitator is to be someone from within the group—and everyone has basic competence in facilitation—it will often not matter who facilitates. If there is an associated presentation, it might be useful to recruit the person whose function or expertise most closely relates to the issue or problem under consideration. In selecting a facilitator from outside the group, you can use the same sort of approach that you would use in hiring someone for any kind of work. Since most outside facilitation is done gratis, either by members of the team's organization or staff from a parent institution's human resources area, there can be a temptation to be thankful for small blessings. Resist this temptation and select your facilitator carefully. Whether you are paying for an outside facilitator or not, here is a checklist of selection criteria that might prove useful:

- ◆ Does the person have previous experience as a facilitator? Can you contact people who will be able to tell you about the quality of the person's facilitation performance?
- ◆ Does the person understand the role and functions of the facilitator, especially the more subtle aspects such as maintaining neutrality and safeguarding ideas? In an initial interview, you might pose a few "what if" questions. What if members disagree about a key issue? What if a group member comes up with a truly outrageous idea that is dismissed by others in the group?
- ◆ Is the person a primary or secondary stakeholder in the issues of the meeting? If your unit catalogs materials and sends them on to special collections, would a person from special collections be able to maintain objectivity? Might they be drawn into an evaluative mode by group members?
- ◆ Does the person have at least as much understanding of facilitation techniques as members of your group? Do they truly know how to conduct a brainstorming session? Would the person be able to read the situation and choose the right facilitation technique?
- ◆ Will they be able to keep the group on track? Do they have the "force of personality" to alert the group that they are wandering away from the outcomes that were established at the beginning of the meeting?

I am not suggesting an elaborate competitive selection process, but I am suggesting that, as in any other skilled work, facilitators can be a good or bad fit for a particular job. Making sure you have the right person can save many hours later on.

Preparing the Facilitator. In many situations, especially when you are using a group member as a facilitator, you will not need to do any special preparation. When you are using an outside facilitator, however, part of the pre-meeting preparation should include at least a brief conversation with the facilitator. Anyone can do this, but it is often seen as an appropriate role for a team leader, department head, or meeting convener. Here is a list of questions about both the group and the task that I tend to use in preparing to facilitate:

- ◆ How large is the group? There is a significant difference in dynamic between a group of four people and a group of fifteen.
- ◆ How well do members know one another? Do they know each other well or will they need to be introduced to each other, to the issues, and to the task?
- ◆ Where is the group in its developmental progress? Forming, storming, norming, performing? Can the group handle conflict in mature ways or is it still learning to disagree? Has it moved into a high-performance mode, where there is a high degree of mutual respect and accomplishment? Each of these stages suggests differences in approach to the problem of facilitation.
- ◆ How effectively do members work together? What is the level of candor in the group? Do they stay on track during discussions?
- ◆ Are members relatively outspoken? Shy? Is there uneven participation? What is the energy level of the group?
- ◆ Does the group get stuck easily? How does it get unstuck?
- ◆ Does the group tend to be happiest when accomplishing a concrete task? Discussing issues or values? Brainstorming? Planning? Exploring theoretical models? Knowing what the group prefers and what it shies away from can be enormously useful to the facilitator.
- ◆ What is the task, the problem to be worked on? What outcomes are needed? Creative ideas? Shared understanding of the issues? A decision? Even though the facilitator may want to work with the group at an initial meeting on their desired outcomes, some exploration of tentative outcomes before the meeting can help shape the process.
- ◆ Is the problem easy or difficult? In designing a process, will you

need to do a great deal of staging work (for example, review of ground rules) before beginning the actual discussion?

♦ How big is the problem—in dollars or in values? Will it require one brief session or several longer sessions?

Practice:

1. Make a list of substantive discussion topics from recent meetings that you have attended. Consider for each topic whether having a facilitator might have helped the discussions. For which topics might you have used a member of the group as a facilitator? For which topics might you have chosen an external facilitator? Why?

2. Conduct an inventory of facilitators who might be available to your group. Who inside the group has the requisite skills? What resources are available through your parent organization? Are there facilitators available in the community outside your parent organization? How much do they charge for their services?

3. The next time you have a substantive discussion requiring full participation by all members of your group, bring in a facilitator to help you with the meeting. After the experience, debrief on it with the group. Was there a qualitative difference in the meeting experience as a result of using a facilitator? Were the benefits worth the additional work of finding and preparing a facilitator? What did you learn from the experience, and what would you do next time you need a facilitator?

ACTION NINE:

Clarify the
Decision Process

How an organization makes decisions—and by extension, how a group within the organization makes decisions in its meetings—is a clear signal for me of the health and effectiveness of that organization. The ninth action, therefore, focuses on decision making: how groups can choose the right decision style, when they should use consensus, and when they should use other kinds of decision methods.

Most literature on effective decision making cites two essential ingredients: *quality* and *acceptance*. *Quality* focuses on the "rightness" of the decision from a technical point of view. For example, if the decision will result in the choice of a very expensive automation system from among several alternatives, the organization and its stakeholders will expect that the *right* system be chosen. The qualitative side of decision making focuses on the rational: what criteria will you use to make the choices? What do the experts, including your resident experts, say? Can you afford your preferred option? The *acceptance* side of decision making, on the other hand, focuses on perceptions and feelings. Will key stakeholders, especially those whose work will be directly affected by the decision, accept and support it? Will they feel they have been sufficiently consulted? Or will they drag their feet, even to the point of slowing or sabotaging implementation?

You must pay attention to both components. If you have a high quality decision—a great decision from a technical point of view—but do not have acceptance, you may be in for a great deal of trouble during implementation. On the other hand, if you have a very popular decision that is technically flawed. you will have problems of a different order, but you will still have problems. In other words: *something times nothing equals trouble*.

There are four basic decision styles, and the choice of style is based on the situation and how important quality and acceptance are. All of the styles are useful, and all of them should be in the repertoire of the group, whether it is an intact work group or a project group. Choosing the right style is a matter of diagnosing the situation. The four decision styles are:

1. *Autocratic.* In the autocratic style, the primary decision maker—whoever has authority and responsibility for making the decision—simply makes the decision, based on her/his knowledge, expertise, and experience. The decision maker may or may not seek additional information from others. The situation calling for such a style is typically one where there is a high need for quality and a low need for acceptance. It is a given, of course, that the decision maker is trusted to do the right thing by those who will be affected by the decision. Autocratic decision making saves time, but there can be a risk in underestimating the need for acceptance.

2. *Consultative.* In this style, the primary decision maker still makes the decision but first consults with others, either one-on-one or in groups. The decision-maker may seek more information, creative input, expert opinion, or visceral reactions from these "consultants." The consultative style is typically used when there is a medium or high need for quality and a medium need for acceptance. But it can also be used when decision makers must stake their jobs or reputations on their decisions. Under such circumstances, it is understandable to most stakeholders that the decision makers would want to reserve the final decision for themselves.

3. *Consensus.* The consensus decision style is appropriate when there is a high to medium need for quality and a high need for acceptance—situations where key stakeholders in the decision not only need to have input into the process but also need to have some control over the final outcome. In true consensus, if there is a primary decision maker, that person sets aside her/his authority and becomes a member of a team making the decision. Consensus

decision making has been the subject of several books and the cause of a great deal of misplaced energy in organizations. Should all decisions be consensus decisions? Does everyone have to agree with the decision? And so forth. It is so rich a topic that it deserves further treatment a bit later in this chapter (see *Consensus 101* below).

4.   *Convenience.* Not all decisions are terribly important. In fact, we make hundreds of decisions every day without involving others in the process. When the need for both quality and acceptance is low, convenience can be the best mode. When I think of decisions of convenience, I usually think of decisions about social events. Where should we hold the team's holiday party? For me, this is a decision that anyone with a rudimentary knowledge of the team could make. However, I understand that my view of when convenience is appropriate may not be shared by others.

Managing the decision process within meetings is not difficult, but it does require constant attention. Here are the recommendations that I offer to my clients:

♦   As part of the process of developing ground rules, discuss decision making. How do members of the intact work group or the project group wish to make decisions? Under what circumstances will it be acceptable to members that convenience or autocratic decisions be made? If the group is focusing on one large decision (which automation system to buy) which will probably involve a number of smaller decisions (such as which vendors to invite to make presentations), it is especially important that decision processes be talked out early in the group's work together.

♦   Even when the group is working on less weighty decisions, it is important to spend a few minutes at the beginning of each "decision episode" talking about the decision process. Who will make the final decision? Which decision style will be used? What is the role of members who won't be making the final decision?

♦ If the primary decision maker is inclined to use the convenience or autocratic style on a particular decision, she/he should consider informing members of this choice, especially if the group is still learning to work together. Though it may seem perfectly reasonable to the decision maker, nothing can destroy the trust that a group has built together like a sudden, highhanded autocratic decision.

♦ Avoid, at all cost, "cosmetic" decision processes. In such processes, the primary decision maker tries to give the illusion of consultation or consensus but, in fact, has already made the decision. There are two very important reasons for not doing this: 1) it doesn't work and 2) you will get caught! Staff in today's work places are too smart for this sort of empty gamesmanship. In addition to the erosion of trust, cosmetic processes can lead to serious implementation problems. If you are going to consult, keep an open mind and really listen to your consultants. If you want a consensus decision, really transfer the decision-making authority to the group. If you are the primary decision maker, most groups will respect you if you say honestly, "Look, I have to make the final decision on this, but I haven't made it yet. I want to hear what you have to say, and I am hoping that you will help me by adding to the information and ideas that I already have. The final decision will probably not please everyone equally, but I know it will be a better decision as a result of your input." They will also respect you if you say, "I have already made the decision. I just want you to know what it is and let me know if there are any fatal flaws in it."

Consensus 101. For many groups, decisions arrived at by consensus are an ideal rather than a daily reality. The extent to which consensus is within the reach of a group depends on the group's definition. The definition I use in workshops describes an ideal goal:

Consensus happens when key stakeholders (the people to whom the decision matters the most) build a decision together that is at least acceptable to and supportable by every member.

The definition implies that when consensus has happened there is enough agreement to move ahead with an action, but typically not unanimous or perfect agreement.

Consensus is one of the most misunderstood concepts in organizations. Some of the most frequently encountered misconceptions follow:

1.   *"Consensus is the same as compromise. You have to compromise in order to reach consensus."* Though consensus often involves being flexible to another's point of view, compromise is really a different kind of process. It often has a mathematical quality which can be heard in a phrase such as, "I met her halfway." It is an expedient process, perfectly appropriate for certain kinds of decisions, particularly those where the stakes are not very high. Compromise is much easier to achieve than consensus and not nearly as effective at building support for a decision.

2.   *"Consensus is something you get other people to do."* Sometimes I have heard leaders describe so-called consensus as something they achieved; they say, in effect, "I built consensus around my idea." While it may be perfectly fine, given the situation, to build support for your idea among key stakeholders, this is really a variation on autocratic decision making. The primary decision maker has made the decision and is simply selling it to potential supporters. Again, few people in today's work places are fooled by such tactics when they pose as consensus.

3.   *"Consensus takes too much time."* Consensus typically takes longer than convenience, autocratic, or consultative decision processes. Whether it takes too much time, however, is very much a matter of opinion. If an organization takes time to make an important decision requiring the support of organizational members and thus assures a greater chance of successful implementation of that decision, isn't that greater certainty of success worth spending time on?

4.   *"All decisions should be made by consensus."* This is the euphoric variation on the cynical response to consensus. Many decisions are more

appropriately made by individuals alone or in consultation with others. Earlier, we explored four basic decision styles: autocratic, consultative, consensus, and convenience, and asserted that all four are appropriate in given circumstances. In general, the greater the need for acceptance of a decision, the more the process should move toward consensus. It is wasteful, however, to spend time on consensus when no one in the group has a strong stake in the outcome.

5. ***"Consensus produces weak, watered-down decisions."*** Many images are conveniently invoked here, including a variety of animals "designed by committees." If consensus is practiced conscientiously, the quality of decisions will actually be higher over time as a result of the synergism that happens in the free give-and-take of inclusive processes. Of course, any process can produce bad results when used badly.

6. ***"Consensus means unanimous agreement."*** This is not a realistic goal for most groups. It can lead to great frustration. As noted above, ideally everyone will agree with, accept, and be able to support a consensus decision. While it can take some time, this is not usually a difficult goal to achieve. Practically, the goal should be that no one leaves a consensus decision session feeling that their concerns have not been heard. They should at least be able to say, "The decision was not the one I would have chosen, but the process was reasonable and fair, my input was considered seriously, and I can accept and support the decision."

Groups need to study consensus and practice it. Practicing it a few times and failing at it does not constitute a fair trial. For most groups, consensus represents a big change—a clear movement away from command and control approaches to shared decision making. Like any new skill, it takes time to learn.

Revisiting Decisions. One of the problems that I hear about frequently from my clients is that groups never seem to leave the decision process. Decisions are continually revisited, sometimes long after they have been signed, sealed, and delivered. In some cases, members honestly appear to believe that by revisiting the decision there might be some hope of reversing or altering it.

Revisiting decisions is a symptom. At its simplest level, it reflects poor decision-making processes. At its most complicated level, it may be a sign that there are far deeper problems such as chronic lack of trust and/or serious ongoing polarities in the group. The more complicated reasons are not the province of this book: re-establishing trust and working through deep differences may take a long time and require professional assistance. Ineffective decision processes, however, can be addressed quickly.

What can you do to reduce or eliminate the revisiting of decisions? Or, how can you improve decision processes so that revisiting is no longer a problem? Many of the answers to these questions have already been presented in this chapter. Here is a brief summary:

- Discuss decision making in general and set some general ground rules. What types of decisions will your group usually make? In what situations is it appropriate for decisions to be made autocratically, through consultation, by consensus, or simply as a matter of convenience? Talk about revisiting decisions and develop ground rules in the group so that members understand when it might be appropriate to revisit and when not.

- Spend at least a few minutes before you move into each decision episode talking about how the decision will be made, by whom it will be made, etc. Be sure that everyone involved understands their roles and responsibilities during the specific decision process.

- Unless there is a very high level of trust in the group, leaders who are inclined to make autocratic or convenience decisions should alert the group when they are going to use these styles.

- Never use "cosmetic" decision processes. Successful decisions depend on everyone acting in good faith and not merely giving the appearance of consultation.

- Record and communicate significant decisions, especially ones where acceptance is an issue. Sometimes decisions are revisited because stakeholders simply do not understand that a decision has been made. Include in the decision record the rationale for the decision and the process that was used.

What if, after you have done everything you can to reduce the revisiting of decisions, a member of the group brings the decision up one more time?

- ♦ When members do revisit decisions, remind them of the group's ground rules. Ask them what they are hoping to accomplish by opening up the decision again.

- ♦ Consult with the entire group. Do they feel that there will be any advantages in revisiting a decision? The objective here is not to allow one member to take the entire group on a revisitation if the group does not want to go.

- ♦ Establish parameters and outcomes. If the decision has been made and is irrevocable, assert this as a boundary. If the revisitation is being proposed as a learning device, set time limits to the discussion and record the results as lessons learned. If the revisitation is being suggested as a means of identifying problems and solving them, structure the discussion as a problem-solving session: identify and describe the problems, brainstorm solutions, evaluate solutions, choose and implement solutions. In other words, revisit with a purpose or not at all. What you want to avoid is an interminable gripe session, especially one fueled by a single person's unhappiness.

Practice:

1. Review the four basic decision styles: autocratic, consultative, consensus, and convenience. How are decisions typically made in your primary work group? How would you divide 100 percent among the four styles? Are you using one style too much or not enough? Remember that all four are appropriate; it depends on the situation.

2. If your group uses consensus, write out a working definition of consensus as your group applies it. Don't worry about making the definition pretty; make it as accurate as possible. Do this in the group if possible.

3. Evaluate your group on its management of decision processes. Do you have decision ground rules? Are roles and responsibilities clear when you are making decisions? Who makes the final decision? Who has input? Do members understand that a decision is being made, how it is being made, who is making it?

4. Develop decision ground rules in your group.

ACTION TEN:

Keep the Meeting on Track

Even in the most efficient and productive meetings, the discussion can sometimes veer mildly or wildly off track. This is normal human behavior. If we were machines, we would keep rigidly to the course and arrive mechanically at the established objective. Being human, we see connections. We are curious. We like to get off the highway and explore the quaint little villages. Endearing though this quality may be, however, we have to get back on course if we are to accomplish our desired meeting outcomes.

ACTION TEN, keeping the meeting on track, is really a hybrid. It involves a number of actions, most of which have already been discussed in this book. If the group is implementing these strategies conscientiously, the incidence of getting off track should diminish significantly. There are also some special actions that you can take to help keep the meeting on track. First, a quick review of the strategies already mentioned:

◆ *The Outcome Agenda.* If you are establishing desired outcomes as part of your planning process for meetings, you are using the single most effective strategy for keeping the meeting on course. If all members participate in the development of desired outcomes, they will be much more disciplined about keeping their attention focused on the task at hand. The outcomes should be posted in a place where everyone can see them. The facilitator or leader can refer to them during the meeting and, when the group begins to stray, remind them of their stated goals. There are occasions when moving off track is appropriate; the group discovers that issue B simply must be dealt with before issue A can be completed. At these junctures the group can make a quick decision to stay off track until the issue is fully dealt with or place it temporarily in a "parking lot" and come back to it at a more appropriate time.

♦ ***Ground Rules.*** If the group has developed a shared ground rule about staying on track, members will be more inclined to recognize when they are veering away and be motivated to return to task. Such a ground rule might look like this: "We will stay on track during our meetings; we will all take responsibility for alerting each other that we are off track."

♦ ***Keep a Visible Running Record of the Meeting.*** Maintaining a flip-chart record of the meeting will help keep the group on track and moving forward. This is especially useful when members want to return to previous topics or repeat points that have been made already. The facilitator—or any member—can refer to the running record and say, "It looks like we've explored that already; is there new information that we need to have?" Or, "We've placed that concern in the parking lot and we'll return to it later."

♦ ***Design the Process.*** As mentioned earlier, many meetings start with a list of topics about which members are free to say whatever they want. No wonder they go off track! If you lay out a process, most members will be grateful. A standard process sequence is to start with idea generation (divergence) and move toward making choices (convergence). This strategy is covered in more detail in **ACTION SEVEN**.

♦ ***Use a Facilitator.*** One function of the facilitator is to act as a traffic cop. Though group members might be blind to what is happening, the facilitator has a more detached view and can see that the group is moving off track. My preferred method of intervention at these junctures is to ask a question or make an "I" statement. "Is this line of discussion leading you to your desired outcome?" Or, "I have a concern about the time and about completing our task today; let's review our desired outcomes for a moment and make sure we'll be able to finish by 4:00 pm."

◆ ***Evaluate the Group's Performance.*** You should spend a few minutes at the end of every meeting evaluating how you performed as a group. If you are having special problems staying on track, be sure to include this specifically in your evaluation. The evaluation might be framed with this question: "How did we do during this meeting in terms of staying on track? Better than usual, worse, the same? What can we do to try to improve our performance in this area?" These ideas should be posted the next time the group meets and reviewed at the start of the meeting.

In addition to these strategies, there are a few specific techniques that can be useful in keeping meetings on track:

◆ ***Reduce the Agenda.*** Just as a cluttered desk seems to invite more clutter, so a cluttered agenda seems to invite getting off track during meetings. Simply put, the more topics you have to talk about, the greater the statistical probability that one of these topics will take you into unexpected and time-wasting directions. If, on the other hand, the agenda is focused on a few outcomes, there will be less of a tendency to move off in many directions.

How do you reduce the agenda? The first step I recommend is to remove or relocate unnecessary ceremonial and informational content. As a library manager, I recall sitting through endless round-robin reporting sessions in which unit heads, put on the spot once or twice a month, struggled to come up with something interesting and engaging to say about their operations. Announcements seemed to clog the beginning of every agenda; sometimes they were important, but more often they were time-fillers. Moreover, most of the content of announcements was already known to participants. And this content—the fillers—came at the beginning of the meeting, taking up precious time that might have focused on solving organizational problems.

Eliminating agenda items requires that you ask a few simple questions:

◆ Does each item really need to be there?

- Is each informational item something that members need to know to do their jobs more effectively? Must the information be communicated in person?
- Could any items be communicated more effectively by e-mail?
- If unit reports or other kinds of meeting ritual are an important means of fostering group cohesion, could you have a special brown bag lunch every once in a while to share such information?

Though you can simply eliminate unnecessary items or relocate them outside the meeting, you can also relocate some of them inside the meeting. This leads to the next idea:

- ***Select the critical items and place them first on the agenda; relocate less important items to the end of the agenda.*** Once you have eliminated unnecessary agenda items, you need to decide which of the remaining items are truly critical and must be addressed during the present meeting. This can be done at the beginning of the meeting by all members, or one or two members can take responsibility for making a preliminary selection and asking the group to review and revise their choices before the meeting starts. The underlying motivator here is perhaps transparent: if members agree in advance to work on the critical items first, and they know ***why*** these items must be dealt with, they will be more likely to stay focused on the task.

- ***Focus each item.*** The Outcome Agenda, as noted earlier, is an important means of disciplining the group process. Outcomes also serve to ***reduce*** the agenda. When you use outcomes, you say in effect, "We are not going to discuss every aspect of this topic; we are committed to discussing only ***this*** aspect and we are moving toward ***this*** outcome."

- ***Prioritize the agenda.*** In complex organizations, I've noticed, everything can begin to look crucially important. And everything can seem to be inextricably related to everything else. When we spend time prioritizing the agenda, we extricate ourselves from this impasse. The key questions to ask are:

- What must we accomplish today?
- Are there deadlines?
- If we are working on a long term project, which specific tasks are in front of us right now?

♦ ***Park some issues.*** Previously, I have mentioned the "parking lot." I have also heard it called a "laundry bag." Whatever you call it, this is an important concept in meeting management. When an issue comes up that is likely to derail the group from achieving its desired outcome, you can put the issue in the parking lot. This means that you acknowledge that the issue is worth discussing ***and*** that you commit to revisiting it at a later time. The group should therefore agree to two things: 1) that the issue is not directly related to achieving the immediate outcomes of the present meeting, and 2) that it is worth revisiting. There does not have to be a lengthy discussion. As a facilitator, I simply ask, "Is this something the group wants to stop and discuss now or can we come back to it later?" Usually the group knows the answer. In practical terms, the parking lot is simply a flip chart sheet headed "Parking Lot." It is posted at the start of every meeting. After a while, the group will get used to this part of the process and individual members will begin to identify their own ideas and the ideas of others as candidates for the parking lot.

♦ ***Manage the parking lot.*** Using the parking lot requires that you commit to revisiting ideas and that you follow through. Sometimes parked issues are resolved during the process of problem solving, in which case simply delete them from the list. Review the parking lot at the beginning and end of each session, asking members if they need to discuss any items now. There is one thing that should absolutely not happen: you should not ignore the parking lot. It is not a sort of dead letter file. Parking and not discussing at some point is a perfect example of "cosmetic process"—process that looks good but, in effect, has a negative effect on the group.

◆ ***Check the time.*** One way to keep the meeting moving is to do periodic time checks. First, always have a clock, in good working order and visible to all members, in the meeting room. Next, at significant junctures (e.g., after an outcome has been achieved) remind the group of how much time has elapsed and how much remains. Though it certainly can be done—and some groups like to work this way—I am not a big fan of setting time limits on agenda items. Usually, in my experience, such limits fail: while you can reasonably time how long it will take to heat a microwave dinner, cooking up a solution to a complex problem is quite a variable process. If you do set time limits, try this technique first: set limits as estimates. If you consistently go beyond your estimates, revise the limits up. The ultimate goal, of course, is not to meet a time limit but to achieve a desired outcome.

Getting Unstuck

Sometimes, the problem is not moving off in unproductive directions. It is not moving at all. The group gets stuck and cannot seem to get unstuck. The first step in getting unstuck is to recognize that getting stuck is perfectly normal. It typically happens when the group is fatigued or when it is trying to "shift gears"— that is, move from one stage of problem solving to another.

Fatigue. One of the themes of this book is that meetings are hard work— especially if the problem being worked on is difficult. Often I facilitate intensive retreats ranging from one to three days. I try to encourage clients not to schedule more than six hours a day, as beyond this limit, in my experience, participants move into exhaustion. Profound fatigue is not likely to happen in short meetings, but it certainly can begin to set in during the second hour of the meeting. I recommend taking frequent short breaks—five or ten minutes per hour—rather than longer breaks. The shorter break should be a time for members to stretch, get some coffee, and visit the restroom. It should ***not*** be used to run back to the office, check on e-mail, return phone calls, or whatever else might interrupt the flow of the meeting. Using the break for these purposes inevitably expands the time—five minutes becomes twenty.

Getting up and moving around will often re-energize the group, but sometimes fatigue just won't go away. In these cases, it might be best simply to adjourn after you have scheduled a time for the group to reconvene and resume the process. There is profound wisdom in the concept of "sleeping on it." I have seen groups make incredible breakthroughs if they just have a bit of time away from the problem. Before adjourning, the group might assign itself some homework—for example, thinking about the problem and jotting down some potential solutions. A caution: don't use adjournment as an excuse for postponing dealing with the problem; schedule the next meeting as soon as possible so you can resume work toward your goal.

Shifting gears. Getting stuck can sometimes be the result of shifting gears. This can happen especially when the group is moving from divergent to convergent processes. Just as the group gets comfortable with generating ideas—just as they have completed a successful brainstorming session and have a great many creative ideas in front of them—they must shift gears and begin the process of sorting through the options and arriving at a final decision. Often members will look bewildered at this point and ask for clarification: "What are we doing?" The first strategy to use when a group is stalled because the gears are shifting is to acknowledge what is happening. The confusion that accompanies a change in process is normal. Then describe the shift in technical terms: "We have spent the last hour generating some very useful potential solutions to our problem. Now we have to focus on our desired outcome and begin to make some choices. Which solutions are really feasible? Which can we afford?" This clarification typically gets the group moving again. If the group stays stuck, it might be time to adjourn and come back to the problem later.

Ask the group. Often the group leader or facilitator feels responsible for getting the group unstuck. The group can take this responsibility on itself, however. As a meeting leader, you can ask the members what they would like to do next.

Facilitator tricks. Getting the group unstuck is something that professional facilitators deal with all the time. There is, in fact, a large body of techniques called "energizers" that are designed to fight fatigue or to bring the group to a suitable level of energy at the beginning of the meeting. Though I use them occasionally, many non-professional facilitators will be understandably reluctant to use them. As a facilitator who will be leaving at the end of the day, I have no qualms about asking members to stand up, stretch, do silly things with their fingers, and repeat nonsense rhymes after me. As someone who has to live with the group, the internal facilitator may have a different view. Nonetheless, if you have the cooperation of the group and feel up to it, energizers can be the solution.

Practice:

1. Review a few recent agendas of your group's meetings. Are there items that are purely informational—items you could have dropped from the agenda? After you have pruned the agendas of informational items, try rearranging the remaining items in order of importance.

2. Next time you meet, introduce the group to the "parking lot." Use it in your meetings for a few months. Then evaluate it as a tool. Did it help keep you on track?

3. Notice when the group gets stuck, when it seems to feel fatigued. Stop the meeting and report your observations. Ask members how they would like to manage these problems. By taking a short break? Postponing the discussion until the next meeting?

ACTION ELEVEN:

Follow Up

Not all meeting problems happen during meetings. In fact, your meetings might seem like a model of efficiency, productivity, and good will. The problems start when there is sluggish follow-up, or perhaps no follow-up at all. This is rather like the hoary dental joke: the teeth are fine but the gums have to come out. If you are not producing the kinds of results that you need after the meeting is over—if you are not getting important tasks done—then the meeting has not really been a success.

Why don't members follow up? The press of other duties, not enough time in the day—these are the standard responses. Indeed, too much to do and not enough time is a complaint I hear frequently in library organizations. I have no reason to doubt the truth of this. My observation has been that our lives in today's libraries have become both more frantic and more frustrating. If, however, the group or specific individual members are having chronic problems with follow-up, it can be a very serious matter. For me, it is not the same as the individual not having the time to complete a project that she alone is interested in and has been working on for years. It is one thing for the individual to be frustrated at not having time to complete a project; it is quite another for a group to feel that a promise has been broken and, in some cases, that process has been used to cheat them. I am not trying to be melodramatic: lack of follow-up on post-meeting tasks is a prime cause of declining morale in organizations and a major symptom of group dysfunction.

This is not a book about fixing chronic performance problems. Short of this level of difficulty, however, there are some strategies the group can use to promote better performance on follow-up. Once again, many of the strategies have been discussed already. If you are using an outcomes approach to agenda setting, your post-meeting tasks are likely to be much more sharply focused. If you are regularly evaluating your meetings, and follow-up is part of that ongoing evaluation, you will soon begin to deal with follow-up problems. Two strategies deserve special review here, however: ground rules and recording.

Ground Rules. There is perhaps no area of meeting management more in need of rules than follow-up. Some days, it is difficult enough to make the rules work when they are posted in front of the group. When members are away from the meeting, how do you make ground rules work? When individual members are back under the pressure of day-to-day work routine, how will they be motivated to follow through on assigned tasks?

Though not a panacea, the ground rules are a way of talking about mutual accountability and establishing the expectation that tasks will be completed as promised. In the very process of developing the rules, each member achieves a clearer, more serious sense of the importance of taking responsibility for following up.

A ground rule about follow-up might look like this:

> "When tasks are assigned to individuals or small groups to be
> completed outside the meeting, it is expected that members will
> take responsibility for completing these tasks on time. If they are
> not able to follow through as promised, members will notify the
> group so that appropriate adjustments can be made."

Make sure the task is clear; then record it. Sometimes the lack of follow-up is as much the fault of the delegators as the members who have been given the task. If you merely ask someone to "do some research on printers and report back to us," unless the person is extremely intuitive you are not providing the clarity they need. You are more likely to get what you need if you spell it out:

> "John, for next time please get prices and specifications on the five
> printers that we've been talking about today and present the
> comparative data in tabular form. All of the information is
> probably available on the Internet at the company Web sites. You
> should also talk with Susan in Systems; she has a good handle on

equipment. If any of the printers cost more than $700, just drop them from consideration."

Then record it. The importance of recording on a visible medium (e.g., flip chart) has been discussed in **ACTION FOUR**. Recording becomes critically important during task planning. One useful technique is to have a simple blank "form" available on a flip chart sheet at the beginning of every meeting. The form will look like this:

What	*Who*	*How*	*By When*

As tasks are identified, they are recorded on the form, so that the completed form for one task might look like this:

What	*Who*	*How*	*By When*
Prepare and present comparison of printer costs and specifications	John	– find data on the Internet – talk with Susan in Systems	9/12/2000 9/15/2000

Recording during the meeting is a way of saying to the members: "We are serious about this and we expect you to perform." The record of tasks can then be transcribed and copies sent to all members.

Here are three additional strategies for improving follow-up:

Review the task list. One of the most important uses of the task list is as a check on progress. Post the group's running task list and review it every time you meet. Cross off items that have been completed; get brief reports on tasks still in progress; identify tasks that are behind schedule and identify the related problems. Occasionally, the review will uncover problems that the group needs to deal with, but they should be mostly minor ones. For example, it might be that the person assigned to the task needs clarification, or the task might need to be redefined in light of newly discovered information.

What do you do when follow-up hasn't happened as expected? If you are keeping a task list and reviewing it regularly in your meetings, you should have fewer problems with follow-up, but there may still be problems. What you want to try to avoid is what seems to happen all too often. A task is assigned with a remote deadline. Weeks or months later, when the task is supposed to be completed, the person responsible confesses that they haven't got around to it yet. Clearly, it is better to discover problems early rather than late. Then the group needs to move into a supportive problem solving mode. It does little good, either in the short or long run, to castigate the member who hasn't made much progress on a task. The first goal should be to get the task back on track by clarifying or adjusting the assignment, helping the person by talking through the task, or even reassigning the task if, because of reasonable circumstances, the person simply isn't able to get the task done. If there is a member with a chronic follow-up problem, either the group leader or the whole group needs to give the person feedback.

Keep the time line reasonable but not too long. I have been in meetings where members have asked to have weeks to complete tasks that might take a few hours at most to complete. Lengthening the time line, while it may appear to be supportive of the person who is taking on the task, actually works against effective follow-up. Many people don't even like to think about tasks until a few days before they are due. Waiting too long to tackle a task means that the task will be less clear when you do get around to it. Moreover, you may be less likely to do a quality job if you are in a panic to get the task done.

Keep the work in the meeting. Though it seems to be efficient to delegate work to be done outside the meeting, it is not always the best way to make sure that work gets done. Jon Katzenbach and Douglas Smith, in their book ***The Wisdom of Teams,*** suggest that one attribute of an effective team is that members "do real work together." In their model, teams spend more time together and depend less on delegation and external follow-up. This has some distinct advantages. Questions of clarity can be dealt with on the spot. Sub-decisions that might hold up an individual's progress can be made quickly. There may be some work to be delegated, but the work will be much easier. Let's look at an example:

The group wants to decide on a holiday reference desk schedule. This task could be delegated to one member with a bit of input from the group. The members then go off and send their individual preferences to the person who has accepted the task. That person struggles to develop a schedule, sends it out to everyone by e-mail, gets their corrections back and revises the schedule, discovers that all the members' preferences cannot be accommodated, sends a revised schedule out again, and finally, after much difficulty, develops a schedule that will be acceptable to everyone. The group could, however, do most of this work in session. Members could bring their calendars and a schedule could be roughed out during the meeting. The work remaining would be simply to "pretty up" the agreed-upon schedule and make a copy for each member without further discussion.

Practice:

1. If you have problems with follow-up in one of your groups, develop group ground rules. Post them in your meeting room and review them very quickly every time you meet. After a month or so, review your progress.

2. Post a blank task list on a flip chart at the beginning of your meetings. When a task develops during the meeting, take a few minutes to write the task down using the ***What, Who, How, By When*** Format.

ACTION TWELVE:

Manage Problem Behaviors

Whenever we think about managing problems in meetings, the focus is almost always on the problem *behaviors* of the people who participate in those meetings. There are, of course, other kinds of problems in meetings, but these are largely technical problems. Equipment might malfunction, an agenda item might need clarification, or the temperature might be uncomfortable. Technical problems are relatively easy to manage. During a meeting I was once facilitating for a client, the electricity failed; we continued to meet by the light coming in through several windows; using flip charts, we accomplished a great deal, perhaps even more than if we had not had to work with this energizing technical failure.

Dealing with each other, however, presents another order of difficulty. It is one of the core challenges of being human. Managing problem behaviors requires three significant shifts in the way we think. First, we need to distinguish the chronically disruptive from the occasionally annoying; the goal of managing meeting behavior is not angelic behavior but a framework of acceptable behavior in which we can get the work of the group done and move toward high quality decisions. Second, we need to focus on behaviors, not on "behavers." Trying to understand why someone behaves badly is an interesting sort of parlor game, but it doesn't usually get us very far. Third, we need to begin to think of the individual's performance in a meeting as no different from performance in other arenas of the job; it is part of the person's work and should be subject to the same performance expectations as the rest of their work.

First, how is problem behavior different from occasional, annoying behavior? All of us have bad days. All of us misbehave occasionally when we are cranky or when something else is absorbing our attention. Most of us tolerate occasional misbehavior in others. Problem behaviors go beyond the normal and tolerable,

99

however. They are both significantly disruptive and chronic. They keep the group from getting its work done, and they occur frequently enough to slow—or stop—progress toward the group's desired outcomes. Knowing the difference between the intermittently annoying and the chronically disruptive is an important step in understanding and managing problem behaviors.

Second, it is critically important to focus on problem *behaviors*, not problem people. This is the focus recommended by most experts on performance. Focusing on the person often leads nowhere and can even result in a worsening of the situation. We spend great quantities of time trying to figure out why someone is misbehaving, as if pinning the motivation down will magically make the problem disappear. While we should always care about people as people, the most effective way to deal with performance problems is to deal with behavior. What is the person doing? What is its impact on the group? What changes do we want in the behavior? When we make this shift, we begin the journey toward solving meeting performance problems.

The third important shift in our thinking is to regard the meeting as a performance arena. There are organizational cultures in which meetings are regarded as somehow separate from—and typically less important than—the "real work" of the organization. And, by extension, one's performance in a meeting does not really count. This is a grand misconception. If you are serious about improving the quality and effectiveness of your meetings, you must begin to see them as no different from the rest of the work of the organization. One's performance in meetings should be viewed in the context of clear expectations, performance evaluation, feedback, and reward systems. Individual members should be just as accountable for meeting performance as for all their other work.

Why are problem behaviors in meetings so difficult for most of us? Why do we avoid dealing with them? The answer is both obvious and perhaps discouraging —dealing with problem behaviors is an unpleasant task. Even the phrase "dealing with" conjures up an unpleasant image: we see ourselves in a confrontation in which we square our shoulders, try to steady our voice, and let the other person know that they are misbehaving. Most people don't want to engage in this sort of unpleasantness. Moreover, most library people prefer introversion: for them, the prospect of such a direct encounter can be especially daunting.

Fortunately, there are other approaches to managing problem behaviors in meetings. If you are using these other approaches effectively, problem behaviors and direct confrontation of them should be exceptional, perhaps even non-existent, events. Most of these strategies have already been discussed in this book. The trick is practicing them.

What does misbehavior in meetings look like? Though human behavior—and misbehavior—can be infinite in its variety, certain behaviors are frequently identified as problems in meetings:

- ◆ ***Dominating the meeting***. Dominators seem to view the meeting as a win/lose situation. They often want their view to prevail, finding it difficult to bend to the ideas of others, so they use a variety of techniques to assert their will. Dominators are often members with some sort of real or assumed authority, and their behavior is an assertion of that authority. A dominator may be a formal leader, a person of long tenure and experience, or someone with specialized expertise. Ironically (for the rest of the group), dominators may be the most vocal advocates of democracy and consensus; they may, in fact, not even realize that they are dominating. Their techniques include a raised voice, a decisive tone of voice, and frequent interruptions (as if the problem-solving process is an annoyance and others should just go along with their view). Their impact on the group is to stifle discussion and move the group, often prematurely, to actions that will have negative repercussions later.

- ◆ ***Talking too much***. Talking too much is, of course, one kind of dominating behavior, but non-dominators can also talk too much. Some people just like to hold the floor. They often get into an unnecessary level of detail or dwell on "war stories" as ways of illustrating a point that other members understood a long time ago. Talking too much is sometimes a sign of insecurity ("If I keep talking, maybe no one will notice that I don't have much to say"). Some talkers are merely highly extroverted, and they are acting out their natural preferences in an innocent manner. Whatever the reason, the person who talks too much can be a source of great frustration in meetings. One problem is that not listening well often accompanies the tendency to talk too much, and active listening—really hearing what the other person has to say—is a fundamental skill in problem-solving and consensus building.

♦ *Holding side conversations*. This behavior can range from an innocent exchange that might grow out of genuine and spontaneous excitement about an idea to disrespectful, passive-aggressive behavior of the most dysfunctional kind. Whatever their motivation, side conversationalists are usually perceived to be disruptive. They distract whoever is currently speaking, sometimes making them lose their train of thought. They often derail, if only momentarily, the process underway. They can cast a negative pall over the meeting. The message of the side conversation is, "Some of us are choosing to stand outside the group and not share what we are doing." Are the side-conversationalists making fun of the proceedings? Are they sharing a secret? Is the content valuable and are they holding back on their contribution? Is the side conversation a passive-aggressive signal that they will not truly support a group decision later on?

♦ *Not participating*. Much of our thinking about problem behaviors focuses on overt behavior, such as holding side conversations or talking too much. The non-participant presents a special challenge—*lack* of behavior is the problem. People don't participate for a variety of reasons. Some are merely shy, but others choose not to participate for very complex reasons. Sometimes, non-participation is learned behavior: members may have discovered over time that when they do participate they are not listened to or they are put down. Or the level of trust may have dropped so far that members express passive-aggressive feelings by being silent. I have observed groups in which non-participants or low-participators make up the majority of members, especially when there are dominating or talkative members. Non-participation affects both the quality and the mood of the meeting.

If members are not participating, the group loses the benefit of their ideas and input, and there is a risk that the quality of the outcome might be compromised. If they are not participating for negative reasons, this is usually clear to the group on some level: it has a negative effect.

♦ ***Challenging, being inappropriately contentious***. Conflict is normal and healthy in a well-performing group. If you never have conflict during meetings, you should worry. The member who is chronically contentious, however, can be a problem for the group. Sometimes members feel it is their duty—their unannounced role—to play devil's advocate. This prompts them to challenge everything, almost on principle. The behavior becomes very irritating for the group, who begin to pay less and less attention to the chronic challenger. This simply makes challengers more challenging as they seek to get the attention of the group. Clearly, the group needs to reach a balance between the kinds of challenges that serve to refine and improve the work of the group and those that merely waste time.

♦ ***Joking, clowning***. While most of us value a sense of humor in the workplace and we all need to take ourselves less seriously from time to time, chronic jokers are irritating because they seem constantly to be devaluing the work of the group. Seeing everything as a joke can be a particularly problem type of passive-aggressive behavior. Jokers might honestly believe that they are serving a useful function in the group. However, the impact of chronic joking on the group can be the perception that the group is being diverted from its desired outcomes.

♦ ***Arriving late, leaving early***. One of the aspects of poor meetings that people most often mention is starting late, usually because all members are not present. For the person who is on time, delaying the start of the meeting is a special irritant. Tardiness can start a destructive chain of thought in other members: "Is that person more important than I am? He seems to be able to break the rules!

I guess maybe I don't have to be on time." And if the group starts the meeting on time, the latecomer often arrives noisily, disrupts the flow of the meeting with profuse apologies, and expects to be brought up to date on what has happened so far. Like clowning, chronic tardiness sends a message that the member is trivializing the meeting and not respecting other members. Chronically leaving early similarly suggests disrespect. The member is saying, "I have more urgent things to do. The meeting is, in effect, over. Don't try to do anything important after I leave."

♦ ***Going off on tangents, getting sidetracked.*** As problem solvers we have two amazing abilities: we can focus our attention and pursue a solution in a logical, linear path, but we can also leap about in our thinking. The latter ability helps us come up with creative options—but it can also send us on wild-goose chases. When members go off on tangents, it may be that they are merely following their natural inclination to see interrelationships among events and ideas. Chronic sidetracking, however, can be a signal that the member is trying to derail the work of the group. The effect on other members is to feel that their time is being wasted. A common form of sidetracking is the "war story"—the extended anecdote that is meant to support a point that the speaker is making. Often, however, the war story does not add value to the discussion; it merely satisfies the speaker's need to be on stage for a while.

♦ ***Interrupting other members.*** Groups have different tolerance levels for interruption. In some high-performing groups where trust is high and meetings are very animated, interruptions are part of the group culture. In most meetings, however, the chronic interrupter disrupts the flow of the problem-solving process, creating for some a climate of disrespect. Interrupting can be a behavior of dominators.

♦ ***Repeating points already made.*** Repetition can be a sub-behavior of talking too much, but it can also be something else. Often the chronic repeater is saying, in effect, "You haven't heard what I've said, so I'm just going to have to say it again and again until you get it." Excessive repetition is seen by many members as another way of wasting time. If you have a repeater *and* a sidetracker in the group, the cumulative effect can be like walking through molasses. Little seems to be accomplished as the group struggles toward its goal.

♦ *Behaving in a passive-aggressive manner.* Passive-aggressiveness underlies many difficult behaviors. In a sense, it is an operating system rather than a specific piece of software. Passive-aggressive behavior is very difficult to pin down and deal with, which is why it comes up so often in discussions of behavioral problems. Literally, passive-aggressive means that the person is taking out her/his aggressions on others—aggressions that can be as strong and nasty as active aggressions—in subtle or passive ways. The active-aggressive typically engages in overt behaviors with clear signals—slamming a book on the table, wagging a finger at another person while yelling at them, exiting abruptly and noisily. While these behaviors can be startling and disruptive, they are much easier to deal with as performance problems than passive-aggressive behaviors. The passive-aggressive sighs, rolls his eyes, shrugs, has a little side conversation, or—subtlest of all—sits perfectly still and declines to participate. The impact on the group can be discouraging, particularly if they feel they need to have the involvement, cooperation, and support of all members.

Why do people misbehave in meetings?

I have a theory: *there is very little evil in the world of work*. Though we may attribute nefarious motives to our colleagues during especially trying sessions with them, it is probably more productive to assume that problem behaviors have a reasonable explanation and then to forget about the reasons and focus on the behavior itself. Nonetheless, a general sense of the varied reasons people misbehave can provide a helpful framework.

Members attend meetings for a variety of purposes. We would like them to attend to help the group in its work of problem solving and decision making. However, in addition to these lofty purposes—and sometimes instead of them—members may be there to assert their authority, to reinforce their sense of belonging, to gossip, to engage in stimulating intellectual debate for its own sake, to take a break from boring desk work, to make sure that history and tradition are honored, to protect themselves and the units they represent (from change, from territorial encroachment), or to sample the pastry and coffee. Everybody is multi-tasking in a meeting. It's human and it's natural. In virtually every chronic misbehavior, you can discover parallel purposes. Latecomers might be trying to impress others with their importance. Talkers might be fulfilling a need for social engagement that is not met in their personal lives. The whole range of passive-aggressive behaviors might be a message to the group: "I am not valued by you and I don't trust you." For the group that is trying to manage behaviors, the goal is to *subordinate* parallel purposes to the major purpose of the meeting: to get specific work done. In an effective meeting, it is this perception—that the group accomplished something worthwhile—that overrides subordinate purposes and allows members to tolerate minor behavioral infractions. Keeping the group on purpose is thus a major strategy for managing difficult behaviors.

How do you manage difficult meeting behaviors?

Earlier, I promised to provide a method of managing difficult meeting behaviors while keeping direct confrontation to a minimum. Here is that method, with the steps you can take. It is not focused on specific behaviors, but when conscientiously applied it will address them all. It involves hard work and continued commitment, but for many people it will be much easier than direct confrontation. Virtually all of these strategies have appeared earlier in this book.

1. *Develop ground rules as a group.* Sometimes people misbehave because they don't know or respect the rules. Or they are playing by a different set of rules than everyone else. An important strategy, therefore, can be to develop the rules that everyone will play by—ground rules, operating rules, or rules of conduct— whatever you want to call them. To make the rules effective, you must also develop a system for implementing them.

The development of ground rules is covered extensively in **ACTION THREE**. Implementing the rules can take the form of a sort of group contract or plan. Who will remind the group and individual members about the rules? The group's formal leader, the facilitator, any member? How will the rules become part of the group's consciousness? Through posting them permanently in the meeting room? Through periodic review? How will you keep the rules fresh and relevant? Developing the rules together and keeping them in front of the group are the most powerful strategies for managing difficult behaviors.

2. ***Diagnose the problem.*** If, after the group has established ground rules, you still have behavioral problems, spend a little time in diagnosis before you move to strategy. The most important diagnostic question for me is, "Is the behavior having a significant negative impact on the ability of the group to accomplish its work?" Another way of asking the diagnostic question is, "Could we cut this person a little slack and allow him an occasional lapse into mild misbehavior, or must we deal with the behavior? Is this behavior truly disruptive, or do I merely find it mildly irritating?"

3. ***Ask all members to take responsibility for implementation of the rules.*** Our natural tendency, when there are rule infractions, is to want someone else to take care of the problem. Though a citizen's arrest is a feature of our legal system, few of us would ever dare to arrest another person. In a meeting, we often want the formal leader or the facilitator to enforce the rules. A much more powerful strategy is for all members to take responsibility for this task. This can be a very difficult step for a group and might be deferred until sufficient trust has been built. As an interim step, asking different members to facilitate and manage the rules for the group from time to time can be effective.

4. ***Keep the group focused on the desired outcomes.*** As recommended in **ACTION ONE**, having the desired outcomes of the meeting identified and posted is a powerful means of keeping the group on task and out of trouble. Desired outcomes send a clear message: "We are here to get work done, not to play games with each other."

5. ***Use effective process design.*** Making conscious choices about process can also be a powerful strategy in reducing or eliminating problem behaviors. If you have

a dominator, a talkative person, or a non-participant, breaking a group into smaller groups for discussions can provide a very simple solution to the problem. Shy participants feel more comfortable in smaller groups. And in a smaller group, the dominator or talkative person will be more inclined to share air time with others. When working with a larger group, using a very structured idea-generation technique such as the Nominal Group Technique, in which everyone writes ideas down and offers them one by one in round-robin fashion, is another very effective means of dealing with over- and under-participation. In virtually all of your design choices, you are moving the focus from the personal and inter-personal to the problem.

6. *Use the flip chart.* Keeping a record of ideas and decisions as you go through the meeting is an effective way of managing some problem behaviors. For example, if you record the repeater's ideas the first time they are mentioned, you can point out that they are now part of the group's memory.

7. *If you must confront a behavior during a meeting, do it in a caring, non-threatening manner.* Always protect the self-esteem of the other person. Refer to the rules. Offer alternatives. If the person is speaking out of turn, ask them to hold their thought. If they are beginning to sidetrack, ask them if their point can be put in a "parking lot" for later discussion.

8. *Confront especially difficult behaviors outside the meeting.* If you are in a position to give feedback to another person on her/his meeting performance (if you are the department head, for example), you will want to handle some problems outside the meeting. Here the process is very much the same as for handling any performance problem, and that is truly the subject of another book. The process in a nutshell, however, follows:

- ◆ Focus on the behaviors, not on the person. Try to describe the problem behavior as clearly and concretely as possible. Avoid discussions of perceived motivation.

- ◆ Describe the perceived impact on others and the impact on you.

- ◆ Listen to the person. Acknowledge what she/he says in rebuttal (the content will probably be defensive). Adjust your own thinking, if you need to, based on the new information that you have. Reassert the need for change in behavior, incorporating that new information.

♦ Work with the person to develop a change focus and an agenda for change. Help her/him identify effective alternatives to the undesirable behavior.

♦ Follow up. Talk with the person at an agreed-upon interval. Present feedback. Has there been improvement? Is the problem still there?

Practice:

1. Review the list of common problem behaviors presented earlier in this chapter. Which behavior is the most problematic for your group? Does this behavior seriously interfere with the work of the group?

2. Now review the list of ideas for managing problem behaviors. Is there a particular strategy here that you feel would address the behavioral problem that you identified above?

Section III: Tools for Improvement

This section of the book provides you with tools for meeting improvement. There are two chapters:

- ◆ **_Checklist: the Whole Sequence._** Section II focuses on twelve actions that you can take to improve your meetings. Those actions are presented in order from easy to more difficult. The Checklist provides a comprehensive look at the steps you might take in preparing for, conducting, and evaluating meetings. It is chronologically organized.

- ◆ **_Job Aids._** The job aids are forms and examples that you might find useful in the process of improving your meetings. They include an agenda form, a task assignment form, a brief meeting checklist, an example of ground rules, and so forth. You have permission to copy all of these pages, as long as you will be using them solely for the purpose of improving your meetings. Any other purpose (e.g., for large-scale training events) requires permission.

CHECKLIST:

The Whole Sequence

In Section II, you read about twelve actions that I believe will make your meetings more productive—perhaps even more enjoyable. In this chapter, I take a linear approach, presenting all the major steps, in chronological order, that you should consider in planning and conducting your meetings.

First things First. Before you actually meet to get your business done, have a meeting about your meetings. You will probably need to do this only once, and it will make a significant difference in the quality of your meetings.

❑ Develop ground rules. Ground rules will help keep your meetings orderly and productive. See **ACTION THREE** for a fuller discussion of Ground Rules.

❑ Have a discussion about how you will typically make decisions. Talking about decision making in general can make your meetings more effective. See **ACTION NINE** for a fuller discussion of clarifying decision processes.

❑ If you have standing meetings, develop a provision for canceling them. If you have nothing urgent to meet about at a regularly scheduled meeting, you will make many friends if you cancel and give participants the gift of time to work on projects at their desks.

❑ Discuss the roles that group members will typically have in your meetings. These roles might include:

- Leader. The person who calls the meetings and conducts them.
- Facilitator. The person who helps make sure that process is as

effective as possible. Sometimes the leader and facilitator functions are carried out by the same person. See **ACTION EIGHT** for a fuller discussion of facilitation.

- Recorder. The person who records ideas, comments, tasks, etc., as they are developed in the meeting. See **ACTION FOUR** for a fuller discussion of recording.

- Participants. Members who do not have one of the roles mentioned above but who participate actively in the discussion and the accomplishment of the desired outcomes of the meeting.

Preparing for a Specific Meeting

❑ Determine the purpose of your meeting. What problems are you trying to solve by having a meeting? What needs are you trying to meet?

❑ Decide whether you really need to meet. Are the purposes of your meeting so compelling that it is worth calling members away from their daily routines? If not, consider cancelling the meeting. Every time they attend a meeting, participants should feel that it is an important part of the work day.

❑ Define the outcomes that you want to have at the end of your meeting. Understanding your desired outcomes will help you shape the content of the meeting and choose the most effective processes. Outcomes are discussed at length in **ACTION ONE**.

❑ Determine the topics you need to discuss to achieve the outcomes that you have defined. To arrive at a specific outcome, you may need to move through several topics. For example, if the desired outcome is to choose a software package from three possibilities, you may identify these topics:

1. Reports on each of the three packages.
2. Discussion of pros and cons.
3. Criteria: what do we need in a software package?
4. Decision.

❑ Arrange the topics in the most effective order. Be sure, for example, to deal first with the topics that you must get through in order to accomplish the desired outcomes. If you rearrange the topics above in logical order, they might look like this:

1. Criteria: what do we need in a software package?
2. Reports on each of the packages.
3. Discussion of pros and cons.
4. Decision.

❑ Determine who needs to meet. The whole group, a small working group, or all key stakeholders? Experts from outside the group? In some organizations, everyone has to meet about everything, which can be a real time-waster for some participants. Talk it over in the group. Perhaps a smaller group can meet, making sure to keep the larger group informed about its work.

❑ Determine whether you need an outside facilitator. Outside facilitators are especially useful when the content of the meeting is going to be difficult for participants or when all members need to focus on the content and cannot be distracted by other duties in the meeting. See **ACTION EIGHT**.

❑ Determine the processes that you will use. For which topics will idea generation (e.g., brainstorming) be appropriate? Where might you use a convergent technique? Which processes will best involve the members of the group during the meeting. See **ACTIONS FIVE** and **SEVEN** for fuller discussions of process.

❑ Identify a facilitator for each part of the meeting (assuming you do not need an outside facilitator). If facilitation skills are well distributed throughout the group, virtually anyone can facilitate most sessions. It can be effective for the person who "sponsors" the item for discussion—that is, brings it to the attention of the group—to be the facilitator. It is not unusual for some groups to have three or four facilitators taking responsibility for different parts of the meeting. See **ACTION EIGHT**.

❑ Determine whether you need someone other than the facilitator(s) to record during the meeting on a medium visible to all participants (whiteboard, flip chart, etc.). Some groups like to have a separate recorder for every meeting. Other groups ask the facilitator to record most of the time and assign someone solely to the recording function on special occasions. Again, the recorder can be anyone in the group, and you may want to rotate this responsibility. See **ACTION FOUR**.

❑ Identify any work that participants should do before the meeting. Should everyone have read specific documents? Do you want members to think about an issue before the meeting? I do not recommend giving participants tons of "homework" before meetings. Many will simply not do it. If there is a significant quantity of information, provide a summary for them.

❑ Estimate the time that specific parts of the meeting will take. For me, setting time limits on specific parts of meetings is not particularly useful. How do you know that a topic won't turn out to be much more difficult to deal with than you predicted? It can, however, be useful to estimate the time the parts will take so that you can determine whether you have enough time to get the work of the meeting accomplished. Plan an appropriate length of time for the meeting based on your estimate of the amount of time that the parts will take.

Organizing the Meeting

❑ Select a meeting location. For many meetings, the location will be fixed—the departmental conference room, for example. Even for these regular meetings, consider changing the location once in a while. If you are meeting to work out some conflicts in the group, it might be good to meet in a comfortable setting away from the library. Meeting in another room in the library can sometimes add energy to the proceedings. The chosen location should, of course, have the resources needed for the meeting—flip chart or whiteboard for recording, audiovisual equipment for presentations, comfortable chairs. See **ACTION SIX** for a fuller discussion of the physical environment of meetings.

❑ Choose a room setup that will be conducive to accomplishing your desired outcomes. Are you going to use smaller discussion groups in the meeting? Does everyone need to see a screen where a slide presentation will be done? See **ACTION SIX**.

❑ Create and distribute an agenda allowing participants time to do pre-work. An agenda format is provided in the Job Aids at the end of this book, but you should feel free to improvise within this format—or invent your own format.

Conducting the Meeting

❑ Start the meeting on time. Not starting on time appears to be *the* most important factor for many people when they express their dissatisfaction with meetings.

❑ Quickly review the results of the evaluation you conducted at the end of the last meeting. What did you say you needed to work on? See **ACTION TWO** for a fuller discussion of meeting evaluation.

❑ Review the purpose, agenda, and outcomes and revise the agenda as needed. Why should you put in all the work that is entailed in constructing an agenda and then open it up for revision as soon as the meeting starts? Often the agenda as pre-designed will be readily approved by all the members. But it sometimes happens that members bring new information to a meeting that will prompt the group to change the order of agenda items or even defer an item to another meeting. This review does not have to take a great deal of time, but it is an important way of saying, "We are going to do some work together, and we want everyone to have a say in what the work will be and how we'll conduct it."

❑ Identify other preliminary activities. Do participants need to be introduced? Do documents need to be handed out? Do roles need to be defined—leader, facilitator, recorder, etc.

❑   If you expect to make decisions during the meeting, determine how they will be made. By consensus? By the leader after she has the input of all participants? See **ACTION NINE** for a fuller discussion of decision making.

❑   Move through the agenda. Though presumably participants will have a copy of the agenda in front of them, post the revised agenda on a flip chart sheet so that everyone can see it. Check items off as you complete them. These simple procedures serve to remind the group that, however tempting it may be to dawdle over a particular item, there are tasks to be accomplished.

❑   Keep the group on track. Remind them occasionally of where they are in the process of the meeting. Remind them of the desired outcomes. If the meeting has wandered off track, intervene as appropriate to remind members that they should move back to the task at hand. See **ACTION TEN** for a fuller discussion of keeping the group on track.

❑   Record as needed, especially outcomes and assignments. Post a number of blank flip chart sheets in the meeting room so that the recorder can record major developments as they happen. This "public" record helps insure that there is follow-up on assignments. See **ACTION FOUR**.

❑   Identify the agenda topics and desired outcomes for your next meeting. A few minutes spent at the end of the meeting planning for the next meeting will take advantage of the energy in the room and save you time later. No one will have to spend hours "creating" the next agenda.

❑   Set the place, date, and time of the next meeting.

Evaluating the Meeting

❑   Use an evaluation method such as plus/delta to assess the performance of the group during the meeting. Identify areas the to work on. These will be reviewed quickly at the start of the next meeting. See **ACTION TWO**.

Conclusion. Reading through all the steps cited above may leave the reader with some distinct impressions. First, a great deal of pre-work goes into a successful meeting. Most of the steps occur before the meeting even starts. The second impression is probably one of exhaustion: so many steps! However, to invoke a hackneyed phrase, meeting management *is* rather like riding a bicycle. The initial experience on a bike involves mastery of many tiny psychomotor skills. With regular practice, what seemed to take forever to accomplish soon becomes routine—you are off and riding without thinking about the micro-skills you are using. Similarly, once you get the hang of it, you will breeze through the meeting management steps.

Practice:

1. Choose a recent meeting that your group has conducted. How many of the steps recommended in the Checklist did you take in preparing, organizing, conducting, and evaluating the meeting?

2. For those steps that your group does not ordinarily use, consider the reason using the list below:

    ♦   It would not add to the effectiveness of our meetings.
    ♦   It would be too difficult for the group to do.
    ♦   It would take too much time.
    ♦   Other reason.

3. Which steps that the group is not presently using would be most beneficial in your view?

4. A two-page meeting checklist can be found on pages 123-124. You may wish to use this checklist as you actually plan meetings.

JOB AIDS

The *job aids* have been developed to help you move from the ideas presented in this book to practical action. They consist of forms, examples, outlines, and a checklist.

All of these tools may be photocopied if you are using them to improve your meetings. For all other purposes, please write for permission.

Though you may find that the aids, as presented, perfectly match your needs, it is more likely that you will want to make adjustments to fit your particular circumstances. You are encouraged to do this.

Here is a list of the *job aids* that follow:

- ♦ Meeting Checklist.
- ♦ Agenda (blank form and filled-in example).
- ♦ Plus/Delta Evaluation Format (blank and example).
- ♦ Outcome-Based Meeting Evaluation (blank and example).
- ♦ Meeting Record (blank and example).
- ♦ Assessment Questionnaire.
- ♦ Meeting Ground Rules (example).
- ♦ Parking Lot (blank and example).
- ♦ Task Worksheet (blank and example).
- ♦ Decision Process Worksheet (blank and example).
- ♦ Decision Record (blank and example).

MEETING
CHECKLIST

Here is a checklist that will help you prepare for a specific meeting. As you are working on improving your meetings, the checklist can also be used as an evaluation tool. Also see the Checklist in Section III.

Planning the Meeting

☐ Make sure that you need to meet—that your work cannot be accomplished in any other way.

☐ Identify and briefly describe the purpose of the meeting.

☐ Develop desired outcomes for the meeting.

☐ Identify the topics that you need to talk about in order to achieve your desired outcomes.

☐ Arrange the topics in the most effective order.

☐ Determine who needs to meet—the whole group or a subset? Should guests be present?

☐ If you need an outside facilitator, make suitable arrangements.

☐ Develop a process plan for the meeting, including idea generation, use of small groups, and other techniques as appropriate.

☐ Identify an internal facilitator for each process phase of the meeting.

☐ If you need a recorder, identify and assign this person.

☐ Identify and assign work that members need to do in advance of the meeting.

☐ Estimate the time that specific parts of the meeting will take.

Organizing the Meeting

☐ Select an appropriate meeting location.

☐ Arrange the meeting room in a way that will be conducive to accomplishing your desired outcomes.

☐ Make sure the room is correctly equipped.

☐ Create and distribute an agenda that allows participants time to do pre-work.

☐ Distribute any other documents that participants might need to accomplish the work of the meeting.

☐ In the meeting room, organize for the recording process. If you are using flip charts, post the flip charts that you will need, including ground rules, parking lot, assignment sheets, and other blank sheets for recording.

Conducting the Meeting

☐ Start the meeting on time.

☐ Quickly review the results of the evaluation that you conducted at the end of your last meeting. Identify the goals you want to work on in the present meeting (e.g., staying on track).

☐ Quickly review the purpose, outcomes, and agenda and revise the agenda as needed.

☐ Determine what decisions need to be made and how they will be made.

☐ Move through the agenda, working from a copy posted on a flip-chart.

☐ Keep the group on track. Track time. Track progress toward desired outcomes.

☐ Record as needed on flip charts. At the very least, record decisions, outcomes, and assignments.

☐ Summarize decisions, actions, assignments.

Ending the Meeting

☐ Identify the agenda topics and desired outcomes for your next meeting.

☐ Select the date, time, and place for the next meeting.

☐ Identify participants for the next meeting.

☐ Evaluate the meeting. Use the plus/delta method or other fast technique. Identify the goals for improvement that you want to focus on the next time you meet.

☐ End the meeting on time.

Post-Meeting Activities

☐ Create and distribute a meeting record , focusing on decisions, actions, and assignments.

☐ Create and distribute a summary of the meeting evaluation.

Group: _____   **AGENDA**

Date: _____

Starting Time: _____

Ending Time: _____

Expected Outcomes:

_____

_____

_____

_____

Topics:

What	How	Who

Pre-Work:

_____

_____

_____

Group: Circulation Services   **AGENDA**

Date: June 16, 2001

Starting Time: 9:30 A.M.

Ending Time: 11:00 A.M.

Expected Outcomes: at the end of the meeting we expect to have:

1. Final decision on hours of opening for July 4.

2. A thorough shared understanding of the new food/drink policy.

3. A list of lessons that we learned from trying the new method for taking reserve requests.

Topics:

What	How	Who
1. Hours of opening on July 4th.	Presentation of proposal, discussion.	Jim, Sandra
2. New food/drink policy.	Presentation, discussion. Tips for enforcement.	Miriam
3. What did we learn from trying out the new reserves procedure? What are the pros and cons of continuing with this procedure?	Nominal group technique census, discussion, next steps.	Clark, Beth

Pre-Work:

1. Read July 4th hours proposal (attached).

2. Read over food/drink policy and bring it with you.

126

PLUS/DELTA EVALUATION

+   ▲

What went well at today's meeting?   What do we need to change?

+   ▲

What went well at today's meeting?   *What do we need to change?*

Mary and Tim: terrific facilitation!   Participation was uneven.

We started and ended on time.   Task planning seemed sketchy.

We achieved our desired outcomes.   The decision matrix seemed to give everyone problems.

OUTCOME-BASED
MEETING EVALUATION

Group: _____

Date: _____

1. We achieved our desired outcomes today. Yes___ No ___ Partially ___

Comments:

2. We were helped in achieving our desired outcomes by:

3. We were hindered in achieving our desired outcomes by:

4. Next time we meet we should:

OUTCOME-BASED
MEETING EVALUATION

Group: Access Services
Date: May 20, 2001

1. We achieved our desired outcomes today. Yes___ No ___ Partially _X_

Comments:

   We got very close to the wording of the new fines policy but did not finish.

2. We were helped in achieving our desired outcomes by:

   1. Everyone was on time.
   2. Greg did a great job facilitating.
   3. Everyone kept their cool and expressed differences in a civilized manner.

3. We were hindered in achieving our desired outcomes by:

   1. Some members talked more than they needed to in order to make their points.
   2. Some members did not talk at all, though I felt they had something to say.
   3. Too many stories, not enough hard data.

4. Next time we meet we should:

   1. Next time we have an issue on which we need to hear from everyone, let's go around the table and do a group census.
   2. Let's do a ground rule about "war stories." They're fascinating but they don't usually contribute much to the decision-making process.

Group: _____   **MEETING RECORD**
Date: _____
Start Time: _____
End Time: _____

Expected Outcomes:

_____
_____
_____
_____

Decisions:

_____
_____
_____
_____

Assignments:

What	Who	By When

Carry-Forwards:

_____
_____
_____
_____

Group: Circulation Services   **MEETING RECORD**
Date: June 16, 2001
Starting Time: 9:30 A.M.
Ending Time: 11:00 A.M.

Expected Outcomes:

  1. Final decision on hours of opening for July 4.
  2. A thorough shared understanding of the new food/drink policy.
  3. A list of lessons that we learned from trying the new method for taking reserve requests.

Decisions:

  1. We'll be open 10:00 to 4:00 on July 4th.
  2. Food and drink policy will go into effect on July 1.
  3. We'll have further training in food/drink policy enforcement in June.

Assignments:

What	Who	By When
Notify Reference and Gov't. Docs. about July 4th hours.	Pam	June 17
See that food/drink signs are made.	Julie	June 20
Schedule training room for f/d training.	Pam	June 17
Write up results of brainstorming on new reserves procedure.	Jim	June 18

Carry-Forwards:

  1. At next meeting, decide whether to continue with reserves procedure.

ASSESSMENT QUESTIONNAIRE

Consider how often each of the following statements is true of your meetings.
Choose **Usually**, **Sometimes**, or **Never**.

	Usually	Sometimes	Never
1. The purpose of our meetings is clear.	_____	_____	_____
2. We have an agenda.	_____	_____	_____
3. The desired outcome of each agenda item is known.	_____	_____	_____
4. Members contribute to the agenda.	_____	_____	_____
5. We have established ground rules.	_____	_____	_____
6. Ground rules are posted and followed.	_____	_____	_____
7. We use a flip chart or whiteboard to record during the meeting.	_____	_____	_____
8. Everyone participates.	_____	_____	_____
9. Our physical meeting space is organized effectively.	_____	_____	_____
10. Our meeting room is furnished with the equipment that we need.	_____	_____	_____
11. Overall, participation is fairly even. No one dominates.	_____	_____	_____
12. We know how decisions will be made and who will make them.	_____	_____	_____
13. At the end of the meeting, members are clear about next steps and tasks.	_____	_____	_____
14. Members follow up on tasks.	_____	_____	_____
15. We meet only when we need to.	_____	_____	_____
16. Members do their homework and complete assigned pre-work.	_____	_____	_____
17. We handle purely informational content outside the meeting.	_____	_____	_____
18. We start and end on time.	_____	_____	_____
19. We use group process effectively.	_____	_____	_____
20. We evaluate how we did at the end of each meeting.	_____	_____	_____
21. We use facilitators, either members of the group or outside facilitators.	_____	_____	_____
22. We accomplish what we need to accomplish in our meetings.	_____	_____	_____
23. We listen effectively to one another.	_____	_____	_____

1. Start and end on time. Don't wait for latecomers.

2. All ideas get a fair and respectful hearing.

3. Do your homework. Come prepared.

4. Speak up. We can't guess what's on your mind.

5. Don't interrupt. Raise your hand when you want to speak next.

6. The facilitator is the keeper of the rules.

7. There are no ranks in our meetings–only smart people with ideas.

8. Everyone in the group is responsible for following up on assigned tasks. Complete them on time or negotiate!

Note: These are examples only. It will be important for your group to develop their own ground rules and to post them for all to see at every meeting.

_____   _____

_____   _____

_____   _____

_____   _____

_____   _____

_____   _____

Discussion of check-in process for serials

Can we hire a temp for the holidays?

New key for the Reference Offices?

Improve custodial services?

TASK WORKSHEET

Group: _____
Date: _____

What is the tasks/assignments?

Who is responsible?

How will the task be accomplished?

By when will the task be accomplished?

TASK WORKSHEET

Group: <u>Reference Department</u>
Date: <u>May 14, 2001</u>

What are the tasks/assignments?

    1. Assess three scheduling software packages and report back to the group.
    2. Report back to the group with recommendation on purchase.

Who is responsible?

    1. John Smith – Web research.
    2. Susan Peters – Call vendors after Web research is completed.
    3. May Simpson – Contact four reference departments using these
           software packages
    4. John, Susan, May – Present report at June 1 meeting.

How will the task be accomplished?

    1. Use criteria established by the group.
    2. Create matrix showing comparative consumer data.
    3. Create brief narrative report of reference department comments.

By when will the task be accomplished?

    June 1, 2001

138

DECISION PROCESS
WORKSHEET

1. Decision to be made:

2. Quality/Acceptance Analysis:

Need for Quality: High _____ Medium _____ Low _____

Need for Acceptance: High _____ Medium _____ Low _____

3. Who will make the final decision?

4. Who needs to be consulted on the final decision?

5. What criteria will be used in making the final decision?

1. Decision to be made:

Holiday desk schedule.

2. Quality/Acceptance Analysis:

Need for Quality: High _____ Medium __X__ Low _____

Need for Acceptance: High __X__ Medium _____ Low _____

3. Who will make the final decision?

All members who will be working on the desk during the holidays will decide by consensus.

4. Who needs to be consulted on the final decision?

Department Head, Access Services, Assistant Director for Public Services

5. What criteria will be used in making the final decision?

Convenience of the library's primary users.

Stay within budget. Avoid hiring temporary librarians to work the desk.

DECISION RECORD

Group: _____
Date: _____

1. The following decision was made:

2. Who made the decision?

3. Process used:

4. Rationale:

DECISION RECORD

Group: Reference Department
Date: June 15, 2001

1. The following decision was made:

To begin implementation of a new information literacy program using the basic framework of hour sessions with students to be held in the library's computer laboratory. See attached program description for details.

2. Who made the decision?

The Information Literacy Task Group of the Reference and Research Department.

3. Process used:

The group developed the program outline and details during sessions in March. They consulted throughout the process with the department head, the Assistant Director for Public Services and the Systems Department. The final decision was made by consensus among Task Group members.

4. Rationale:

Data gathered over the last two years indicated a compelling need for this program.

INDEX

M

Maintenance skills, 14–15
Meetings
   :basic concepts, 11–17
   :conducting, 117–118
   :diagnosing, 9, 19–29
   :evaluating, 28, 31–32, 37–41,
       87, 124
   :facilitating, 29, 69–73, 86–87,
       91–92, 113–114, 115–116
   :follow-up, 31, 93–97
   :organizing, 116–117, 123–124
   :purpose of, 25, 106, 117
   :recording, 25–26, 47–50, 116,
       117, 118, 124, 131–132,
       141–142
   :staying on track, 26, 34, 69,
       85–92, 96, 118
Minutes: see Meetings: recording

N

Nominal Group Technique, 54–55
Non-participation in meetings, 51,
    102–103

O

Outcome agendas, 25, 33–36
Outcome-based evaluation, 40–41,
    129–130

P

"Parking lot," use of, 85–86, 89–90,
    135–136
Participation, 16, 26, 51–57,
    102–103
Physical environment, 26, 59–62,
    116–117
Plus/delta evaluation, 39–41,
    118–119, 127–128

Process, designing, 28, 63–68, 108

R

Rules: see Ground rules

S

Seating, 60–61
Separating process parts, 63–68
Standing meetings, 13
Subgroup, 16, 55–56

T

Task skills, 14–15

FURTHER READING

Bianchi, Sue, et al. *Warmups for Meeting Leaders.* San Diego, Pfeiffer and Company, 1990.

Bradford, Leland. *Making Meetings Work.* La Jolla, California: University Associates, 1976.

Butler, Ava. *TeamThink: 72 Ways to Make Good, Smart, Quick Decisions in Any Meeting.* New York: McGraw-Hill, 1996.

Cheng, Richard Y. and Kevin R. Kehoe. *Meetings That Work!* Irvine, California: Richard Chang Associates, 1994.

Dewey, Barbara I. and Sheila D. Creth. *Team Power: Making Library Meetings Work.* Chicago: American Library Association, 1993.

Doyle, Michael and David Straus. *How to Make Meetings Work.* New York: Jove Books, 1976.

Haynes, Marion E. *Effective Meeting Skills.* Menlo Park, California: Crisp Publications, 1997.

Michalko, Michael. *Thinkertoys.* Berkeley, California: Ten Speed Press, 1991.

Rees, Fran. *The Facilitator Excellence Handbook.* San Francisco: Jossey-Bass/Pfeiffer, 1998.

Rees, Fran. *How to Lead Work Teams.* San Diego: Pfeiffer and Company, 1991.

Rees, Fran. *Teamwork from Start to Finish.* San Francisco: Jossey-Bass/Pfeiffer, 1997.

Saint, Steven and James R. Lawson. *Rules for Reaching Consensus.* San Diego: Pfeiffer and Company, 1994.

Tagliere, Daniel A. *How to Meet, Think, and Work to Consensus.* San Diego: Pfeiffer and Company, 1993.